To

RITA

and

JENNIFER, PHILIP, PAULA and

TESSA

ECONOMICS
AND
INSURANCE

An Introduction to the Economic Aspects
of Insurance

By

R. L. CARTER, B.Sc.(Econ.), D.Phil., F.C.I.I.

Dept of Industrial Economics
University of Nottingham

PH Press Ltd., Waterloo Road, Stockport, Cheshire

PREFACE

The original intention of this book was to cover the economics section of the subject "The legal and economic aspects of insurance" which forms part of the qualifying examinations of the Chartered Insurance Institute. It is hoped, however, that it will also prove to be of interest to two other groups of readers. First to other students of economics or business studies who either wish to know more about the role of insurance in the economy and its management problems, or are looking for an applied economics textbook covering a service industry. Second there are those managers in the insurance industry itself who are concerned with planning, and decisions regarding pricing and allied subjects, and for whom economic analysis offers a powerful tool.

After describing the size and organisation of the industry, the book has two main aims. First it seeks to analyse and explain the role of the industry and the influence its operations have on the British economy. Then it provides an introduction to the application of economic analysis to the problems of insurance management. In this last section, although it draws on economic theory, sufficient explanation has been provided to make the work intelligible to readers who have not already pursued an economics course of study.

In writing this book I have received much help from colleagues at the University of Nottingham, and I should like to record my gratitude for their comments and guidance. In particular I especially wish to thank Messrs. J. M. Bates and J. F. Lowe for their help, and Mr. B. Chiplin who critically read a large part of the original draft. Also I must mention the assistance I received from the industry and in particular for Mr. J. B. H. Pegler's discerning comments regarding the industry's investment behaviour. Much of the credit must go to them; any errors or omissions which remain are mine alone.

Finally I gratefully express my thanks to Mrs. Margaret Genway for helping to decipher and type a large part of the manuscript, and to my wife and children, without whose encouragement and forbearance nothing would have been possible.

R.L.C.

CONTENTS

INTRODUCTION

Judged by any standards the insurance industry plays a major role in the economy of the United Kingdom. It enables individuals and firms to obtain financial security against many of the risks which beset everyday life; it provides a major source of long-term capital; and it is the largest net contributor to the country's invisible overseas earnings. It has, however, largely been ignored by economists. Consequently few students of economics have any clear understanding of the operations of the industry, and generally for its part insurance management has tended to overlook economic analysis as a tool for better decision-taking. It is hoped that this book will help to remedy some of these defects.

The first part of the book is devoted to a brief description of the development, size and organisation of the industry. As the reader will soon discover, the organisation of the industry is highly complex and serves a wide variety of buyers ranging from international corporations to individual consumers. Therefore, rather than treating it as a single homogeneous unit it is more meaningful for many purposes to regard it as a group of firms all involved in the handling of risks but operating in a series of interrelated markets. Unfortunately, however, economic analysis along such lines is impeded by the lack of detailed statistical data despite the apparent wealth of material published each year by the industry. Nevertheless Part I provides the basic type of information required to progress to the problems discussed in Parts II and III.

Part II examines the role of insurance in the economy under the three headings mentioned above. Apart from the industry's investment operations, it is surprising how little research has been undertaken into many of the vital questions raised by its activities. For many generations the industry was content to operate along well-trodden conventional ways. Today it is being forced to readjust to rapidly changing economic, social and political conditions, some of which call into question its continued existence in its present form. On the other hand even countries with state-controlled, planned economies have found it desirable to retain an insurance industry.

Finally Part III seeks to provide an introductory economic analysis of the primary function of the industry; that is, its handling of risks. The sub-title to this Part, "Analysis for decision-taking", explains the object, which is to show how economic concepts and techniques may be used to improve the quality of the decisions taken by insurance management. Although the reader is assumed to have no prior knowledge of economics, obviously anyone who has already studied economic theory will find it easier to follow some of the analysis. Likewise although a few mathematical proofs are given these should not present any difficulties for anyone familiar with "O" level algebra.

It must be emphasised that Part III in particular only provides an introduction to the subject. References to more advanced works are provided for readers interested in pursuing specialist topics in greater depth, and additional general reading is suggested at the end of the last chapter.

Finally a word for the unwary regarding the nature of economic theory, which is a vast and developing subject. Most theories are based on deductive reasoning and though a theory may be logically sound it cannot be regarded as completely valid until it has been thoroughly tested empirically. Few economic theories have fully passed such a test (and in some cases by the very nature of the theory and/or its underlying assumptions such testing is impossible) so that generally economic theories cannot provide an absolutely certain basis for predicting the future. Nevertheless even theories which are based on largely or wholly untested hypotheses may provide a better guide for decision-taking and corporate planning than an approach totally lacking in theoretical analysis.

R.L.C.

PART I
THE INSURANCE INDUSTRY

Chapter 1

The concept of an industry lends itself to a variety of definitions usually based upon some common factor applicable to a collection of firms. So, for example, an industry may be defined in terms of a collection of firms engaged in the production of closely competing products, or sharing common problems arising out of the usage of the same raw materials or methods of production.

Therefore the first task must be to define what is meant by the insurance industry for the purpose of this book. A glance at table 1.1 will show that there are a large number of firms involved in the

Table 1.1
Structure of the UK Insurance Market—1968

	U.K. registered	Foreign Companies	TOTAL
INSURERS:			
Companies writing only life & personal accident business ..	93	25	118
Companies writing only general business	146	106	252
Companies writing only life & general	30	6	36
	269	137	406(1)
Lloyd's			
Marine, plate glass, & other specialist non-life mutual associations & companies	161	—	161
Collecting societies	74	—	74
Other friendly societies	796	—	796
INTERMEDIARIES			
Brokers			
(a) firms belonging to the associations (approximately) ..		2,000	
(b) other firms (estimate) ..		4,000	
Part-time agents (estimate) ..		120,000 (2)	

Source: Insurers— Board of Trade "Insurance Business" Statistics Sept·
1966 to Aug. 1968.
Report of the Industrial Assurance Commissioner, 1968
Annual Abstract of Statistics 1970.
Brokers— The Lloyd's Insurance Brokers' Association
The Corporation of Insurance Brokers
The Association of Insurance Brokers
The Federation of Insurance Brokers

Note (1): In addition there were 6 foreign companies and 121 U.K. companies (including 92 subsidiary companies) for which separate accounts had not been submitted to the Board of Trade.

Note (2): In 1971 the Economist Intelligence Unit estimated that the six principal types of agent—solicitors, accountants, bank managers, building societies, estate agents and garages—have a potential of around 72,500 sales outlets. "Insurance profile of an industry" published by the Corporation of Insurance Brokers (1971).

handling of insurance in the United Kingdom, including both the companies, societies and individuals underwriting insurance business and the intermediaries engaged in its marketing. In this book it is proposed to concentrate primarily upon the former group, and more particularly the companies and Lloyd's which are producing closely competing services. However, this does not mean that the remainder of the firms and societies operating in what may be vaguely called "the insurance market" can be ignored entirely. As can be seen from figure 1a, which presents a simple organisation chart of the industry, the brokers, for example, obviously have an important influence on the competitive situation and therefore will be one of the factors considered when competition is discussed.

A definition of insurance

The basic function of insurance is to provide protection against the financial losses arising from the occurrence of pure risks. It is a process of risk transfer whereby the individual, firm or other organisation exposed to the risk can, in return for the payment of a premium, transfer to an insurer the risk of financial loss resulting from the occurrence of a specified event.

This concept of insurance was succinctly expressed in the preamble to the first Act to regulate insurance in England, which explains that:

> ". . . by means of which policies of assurance it cometh to pass on the perishing of any ship, there followeth not the undoing of any man, but the loss lighteth rather easily upon many than heavily upon few . . ." [1]

Obviously only the risk of the financial loss is transferred to the insurer; insurance cannot prevent loss, damage or injury occurring to the subject matter of the insurance itself, i.e. to the life, property or other interest insured. Also insurance can only offer protection against those economic losses which are determinable and can be measured in monetary terms. Dr. A. H. Willett pointed out that one of the limitations of insurance is that it does not compensate for what he called the personal risks, e.g. the suffering resulting from injury, or the loss of commodities possessing sentimental values far beyond their values in exchange. [2]

Allowing for these qualifications Professor I. Pfeffer therefore defined insurance as:

> ". . . a device for the reduction of the uncertainty of one party, called the insured, through the transfer of particular risks to another

---

[1] "Act touching policies of assurance used among merchants, 1601"— see H. E. Raynes *A History of British insurance* 2nd edtn. p53. Pitman (1964).
[2] *The theory of risk & insurance* 1901 reprinted by University of Pennsylvania Press 1951 p12.

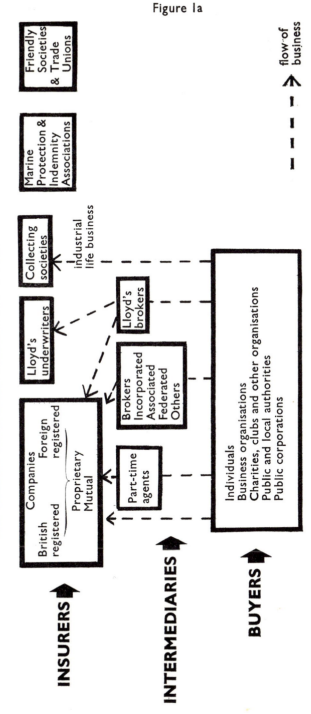

The British Insurance Market for direct business

flow of business

INSURERS

Companies
British registered   Foreign registered
Proprietary   Mutual

Lloyd's underwriters

Collecting societies

industrial life business

Marine Protection & Indemnity Associations

Friendly Societies & Trade Unions

INTERMEDIARIES

Part-time agents

Brokers
Incorporated
Associated
Federated
Others

Lloyd's brokers

BUYERS

Individuals
Business organisations
Charities, clubs and other organisations
Public and local authorities
Public corporations

Note I: Lloyd's and most of the companies also handle reinsurance business both between themselves and with foreign companies throughout the world, so providing a complex network for spreading large risks throughout the world's insurance markets

party, called the insurer, who offers a restoration, at least in part, of economic losses suffered by the insured". [3]

This, then, is the basic product which the insurance industry supplies. Over the years, however, insurers have added other services. For example, a substantial part of life business is concerned with various types of savings contracts, and inspection services to comply with the requirements of the Factories Acts form a major part of engineering insurance business.

The size and growth of the industry

The post-war development of British insurance companies and Lloyd's is summarised in table 1.2. By 1968 their total premium

Table 1.2
World-wide premium income of British insurers

	1945 £	1955 £	1965 £	1968 £	£ thousand Growth rate 1955-68 % p.a.
	(a) UK registered companies				
Ordinary life & annuities	117,496	331,000	849,292	1,224,754	10·6
Industrial life	79,392	127,408	204,009	234,821	4·8
Total life	196,888	458,408	1,053,301	1,459,575	9·3
Fire	71,777	218,914	368,161	500,307	6·6
Accident (non-motor)	56,967	258,844	336,143	481,433	4·9
Motor	33,828	180,505	478,166	598,306	9·6
Marine & aviation	22,618	65,448	104,439	210,341	9·3
Total non-life	185,190	723,711	1,286,909	1,790,387	7·2
Total	382,078	1,182,119	2,340,210	3,249,962	8·1
	(b) Lloyd's				
Life	N.A.	44	393	700	23·6
Fire & accident	N.A.	118,695	257,676	342,320	8·5
Motor	N.A.	8,166	27,190	36,510	12·2
Marine & aviation	N.A.	105,525	176,138	288,690	8·1
Total non-life		232,386	461,004	667,520	8·5
Total		232,430	461,397	668,220	8·5

Sources: Annual Abstracts of Statistics, Lloyd's

Notes:
The companies' marine and all Lloyd's premiums are net of brokerage and commissions

income was equal to over 10½ per cent of the Gross National Product (GNP), and the indications are that this figure will continue to rise.

Since the early 1950's, despite inflation, most peoples in the western world have enjoyed the benefits of technological progress and, in consequence, rising living standards. The insurance industry has shared in that progress with premium incomes in many countries growing much faster than their GNP's. The rising demand for motor insurance consequent upon the spread of car ownership is perhaps the most obvious example of the way in

---

[3] *Insurance & economic theory*. R. D. Irwin Ince (1956).

which the insurance industry has benefited. However, in industry and commerce the general expansion of economic activity combined with new products and methods of production has not only led to an increase in the number and/or size of exposure units but has also created a demand for insurance against new types of risk. Rising real incomes also tend to lead to higher levels of personal saving in which life insurers and the pension funds have been able to increase their share of the total. Being major exporters of insurance services, British insurers have been able to participate in such growth of demand both at home and abroad. Despite economic nationalism which has impeded their overseas business, over two-thirds of the general insurance business of the companies and Lloyd's, and almost one-eighth of the companies' life premiums, are earned abroad.

Unfortunately a detailed geographical analysis of the growth of the industry's business is impossible because of lack of published data. Before 1967 a precise separation of home and overseas business is available only for life insurance, for which details are given in table 1.3. The slower growth rate for UK life premiums is attributable partly, but not wholly, to the inclusion of industrial life business.

Table 1.3
Life premium income of British insurers
and the Gross National Product

	1955 £ million	1968 £ million	Average annual growth rate %
UK life & annuity premiums of British insurers	419	1,285	9·0
Overseas life & annuity premiums of British insurers	39	174	12·2
UK Gross national product at factor cost (current prices)	16,078	36,819	6·6

Source: Annual Abstract of Statistics

Although the growth of premium income has been faster in some of the other countries of western Europe, the general picture presented by tables 1.2 and 1.3 is of an industry expanding more rapidly than the economy in general.

The two tables, however, make no allowance for the continuous rise in prices which occurred over the period, which reduced the real annual growth rate of the UK economy from 6.6 per cent to approximately 2.7 per cent. If a comparison of the real growth rates of the economy and the industry is required then the premium income figures likewise need correction to eliminate the effects both of inflation and of the two devaluations of 1949 and 1967. Given details regarding the geographical distribution of overseas premium income a reasonably accurate devaluation factor could be calculated, but any attempt to isolate the effects of inflation on premium income from the changes in other determinants over the years would be an extremely complicated, if not impossible, task. For example, it would be necessary to ascertain what proportion of the rise in motor premium income could be attributed to increases in (i) the number of vehicles insured; (ii) the number of motorists effecting comprehensive rather than third party only insurance; (iii) the frequency of claims; (iv) the numbers of seriously injured who now survive as a result of improved medical knowledge; (v) changes in car design and repair techniques; and so forth.

The structure of the industry

The present structure of the British insurance industry is the result of a process of development extending over more than three centuries.

In 1601 insurance business in Britain virtually was restricted to merchants and shippers seeking protection against the loss of their goods and ships at sea from a market consisting of a limited number of individual merchant underwriters operating in the Royal Exchange and the coffee-houses of London. Life assurance was in a very crude and early stage of development, while another 79 and 239 years respectively were to pass before the first fire and accident insurance policies were issued in London [4].

Today Lloyd's remains as the survivor of that original 17th-century system of individual merchant underwriters. Its 6,000 underwriting members now transact their business through some 300 syndicates managed by professional underwriters but each member remains individually liable for his share of any risk accepted by the syndicate [5].

The first companies to appear in the market were formed after the Fire of London. The longest survivor was the Hand-in-Hand, established in 1696 and acquired by the Commercial Union in 1905. Shortly afterwards, in 1720, the Royal Exchange Assurance and the London Assurance were incorporated by Royal Charter and given a monopoly of corporate underwriting of marine insurance. So were laid the foundations of the company market.

The system of agency representation is of equally long standing. Access to a Lloyd's underwriter traditionally has been through a broker, and today only the firms belonging to the Lloyd's Insurance Brokers' Association (269 in 1969) have the right to enter the Underwriting Room to place business on the Lloyd's market. Outside Lloyd's the role of the full-time expert insurance broker is largely a 20th-century development, but by the turn of the 19th century the growing insurance companies were achieving countrywide representation through the appointment of part-time agents in principal towns.

At the end of 1969 the Insurance and Companies Department of the Department of Trade & Industry reported that there were

---

[4] See H. E. Raynes, *op cit*.
[5] For an account of the history of Lloyd's see D. E. W. Gibb *Lloyd's of London*. Macmillan & Co (1957).

727 British and foreign registered companies and mutual associations authorised to carry on one or more classes of insurance business in Great Britain. These can be further analysed as follows:

Table 1.4
Companies authorised to transact insurance business in the UK at 31 Dec '69

Companies transacting:	British registered companies	Foreign registered companies
Long-term (i.e. life) business only ..	178	35
Long-term & other classes of business	579	148

Source: *Insurance Business* 1969

Comparison with table 1.1 shows, however, that the industry is far less dispersed than these figures suggest. Mutual associations account for over 150 of the total number; these largely comprise very small local bodies insuring plate glass windows, and the Protection and Indemnity Associations (some having premium incomes exceeding £1 million per annum) covering risks for shipowners which are not insurable by normal marine policies. Also, as shown in the footnote to table 1.1, the large insurance groups account for well over 100 subsidiary companies whose underwriting policies generally are closely controlled by their parent companies. Therefore the effective number of independent units in the industry, as defined above, is approximately 400 companies plus Lloyd's.

Effectively the industry today is dominated by about fifteen companies plus Lloyd's. This situation has partly arisen from a series of mergers through which 22 of the leading non-life companies operating independently in 1956 had been combined into 7 groups by December 1968. The result has been to increase the level of concentration in the industry as shown by table 1.5, size

Table 1.5
Changing market shares of British insurers based on their total world-wide fire & accident premium incomes

	1956	1963	1968
3 largest companies	27·2%	32·9%	40·4%
6 largest companies	38·8%	47·9%	57·1%
12 largest companies	55·0%	64·7%	68·7%
Lloyd's	20·9%	21·1%	19·2%

Source: compiled from Annual Summaries of Accounts & Statements of Insurance Business. H.M.S.O.

being measured by premium income. In the marine and aviation markets Lloyd's accounted for 57.5 per cent of total premium income in 1968 with the 6 leading insurance groups controlling 19.1 per cent.

Similarly in 1968 the three largest ordinary life companies underwrote almost 28 per cent of the premium income of British companies, and in industrial life the three largest companies accounted for 54 per cent of the premium income of both the companies and collecting societies.

Lloyd's very small share of the life market is due to Lloyd's underwriters having been excluded from transacting long-term life assurance business because of their lack of corporate status. Following a report by a committee under Lord Cromer, the Committee of Lloyd's decided in 1971 to acquire a life company but their first attempt (to take over the Lifeguard Assurance Company) failed on the question of price. Later that summer it was decided to establish an entirely new company.

Foreign insurance companies are less important in the British market than their numbers suggest. Many are represented in London purely in order to transact reinsurance business [6] and relatively few underwrite a substantial volume of British business. Returns submitted to the Board of Trade showed that in 1965 only nine foreign registered companies (three Australian and six Canadian) had an annual UK life premium income exceeding £1 million; for non-life business the position was as follows:

Table 1.6
Foreign Insurance Companies operating in Britain

Country of registration	Number of companies with UK general premiums exceeding £250,000 in 1965
Australia	2
Canada	2
West Germany	1
India	2
New Zealand	2
Switzerland	4
United States	2

On the other hand the interest of foreign insurers has been increasing, as is evidenced by the numbers of new entrants to the market, and is likely to continue to do so. Also a number of British registered companies are wholly or partly owned by foreign insurers; for example, the Bedford General is a subsidiary of the Swiss company, the Zurich, and the Continental of New York owns a quarter of the issued share capital of the Phoenix Assurance Co., the sixth largest British composite company.

Types of company: Insurance business can be divided into different classes. Until recently the conventional classification was into fire, accident, marine and life business, but with the encouragement of the Companies Act 1967 it is now becoming more usual to distinguish between property; liability; motor vehicle; pecuniary loss; personal accident; marine, aviation and transit; long-term; and industrial (life) assurance business. One feature of the industry has always been the presence of specialist companies

---

[6] Reinsurance is a method whereby one party, known as the reinsurer, agrees in return for a premium to accept all or part of a risk which has been insured by the other party, known as the ceding company.

transacting only one main class of business.

Such companies are particularly important in the long term (i.e. ordinary life assurance) and marine markets where respectively they control approximately 40 per cent and 15 per cent of total premium incomes. Conversely most of the major companies have developed into composite groups transacting all classes of insurance business, so possessing the advantage of being able to offer the public a comprehensive insurance service.

The life market is also notable for the number of companies organised on a mutual basis where the policyholders are the owners of the company, and those who have effected with-profit policies receive all of the surplus revealed by the periodic valuation of assets and liabilities. In general business, in addition to the plate glass and marine mutual associations noted above, there are a small number of mutual companies formed mainly to underwrite the business of firms operating in certain trades. Altogether such mutual companies control approximately 3 per cent of the total general (non-marine) premium income of British insurers.

In recent years conversion to a mutual organisation has been seen by a few of the smaller life offices as a means of avoiding possible take-overs, the purchase of a proprietary life office being a cheap way of acquiring control over substantial funds.

Market organisations

A noteworthy feature of the industry's organisation is the development of market associations, which have had a significant influence on competitive behaviour.

Such associations have been and still are particularly important in non-life business. All were formed at times when intense competition threatened the stability of the market and the security which could be provided for policyholders [7].

Foremost is the Fire Offices' Committee, formed in 1868 to regulate premium rates at a time when price-cutting was bringing about the failure of many companies. Records show that between 1850 and 1899 at least 399 companies were wound up and another 419 were taken over by other companies [8]. In 1906, following the enactment of the Workmen's Compensation Acts, insurance companies anxious to provide employers with uniform rates and conditions, and secure insurance arrangements, sought to achieve this end through the establishment of the Accident Offices' Association, followed by the Engineering Offices' Association, in 1920. Most of the major companies and many of the smaller ones, but not Lloyd's, joined all three bodies.

These tariff associations mainly influenced competition through

---

[7] See B. Supple *The Royal Exchange Assurance*. Cambridge University Press (1970).
[8] *Insurance Directory & Year Book* 1964-65. List of Companies wound up; Amalgamated companies and Allied companies.

their agreements on minimum premium rates for different classes of fire, consequential loss, motor, employers liability, engineering and certain types of livestock and fidelity guarantee risks. The rates were based on loss statistics pooled by the members, plus a loading for commission, expenses and profit apparently representative of the costs of an average member company. Theoretically the rates were subject to regular revision, but before mounting UK fire losses forced the companies in December 1963 to impose a 15 per cent surcharge on fire premium rates for most industrial and commercial properties, the Fire Offices' Committee had collected the experience of members only on an *ad hoc* basis when a member had called for a review of the tariff[9].

Besides controlling premium rates the tariff associations also regulated policy wordings and the rates of commission paid to brokers.

The relative importance of the three bodies in the fire and accident markets is shown in table 1.7, although if it were possible to

Table 1.7

Market share of world-wide premium income of British insurance companies (excluding specialist reinsurance companies)

	1928 Premium £m	%	1938 Premium £m	%	1948 Premium £m	%	1956 Premium £m	%	£ million 1966 Premium £m	%
Company fire premiums										
Total	60·2		49·7		125·3		249·9		392·9	
Tariff companies	57·2	95·0	46·4	93·3	116·2	92·7	223·9	89·6	322·4	82·1
Non-tariff ,,	3·0	5·0	3·4	6·7	9·1	7·3	26·0	10·4	70·5	17·9
Company accident premiums										
Total	65·3		78·4		154·3		390·4		837·1	
Tariff companies	51·3	78·6	56·0	71·4	112·0	72·6	284·4	72·8	587·4	70·2
Non-tariff ,,	13·9	21·3	22·4	28·6	42·3	27·4	106·0	27·2	249·7	29·8

Sources: The *Insurance Shareholder's Guide* 1929-30
Assurance Companies Returns 1929
,, ,, ,, 1938
The *Policy Holder Year Book* 1939-40
,, ,, ,, ,, ,, 1949-50
Summary of Accounts & Statements deposited with the Board of Trade during year ending 31.12.49
,, ,, ,, ,, ,, 31.12.59
Policy Holder fire & accident tables for 1958
Policy Holder fire & accident tables for 1966

separate UK and overseas business the non-tariff share of the UK market alone probably would prove to have been a little larger than is suggested by the world-wide figures. In addition Lloyd's provided substantial additional non-tariff competition; between 1928 and 1966 it was able to increase its share of combined fire and accident premiums from 11.4 per cent to over 20 per cent but in the later 1960's it slipped back a little owing to limitations on its capacity to absorb large risks.

In October 1968 it was announced that the supply of fire insurance was to be referred to the Monopolies Commission which

[9] See R. L. Carter *Competition in the British fire and accident insurance market* (1968). Unpublished D.Phil thesis, University of Sussex.

amongst other things would investigate the working of the Fire Offices' Committee. Three months later the members of the Accident Offices' Association announced that they proposed voluntarily to end the regulation of accident premiums, dealing first with motor insurance from the 31st December 1968 and ending with engineering insurance on 31st December 1970. In 1970 the F.O.C. decided to terminate the household tariff as from 31st December 1970. Therefore only industrial and commercial fire and allied risks now remain subject to tariff regulation.

The reasons for ending such long-standing arrangements seem to have been two-fold. Firstly the independent companies and Lloyd's had been able to exploit the weaknesses of the tariff system to increase their shares of the market. This particularly applied to motor insurance where by 1968 the tariff companies' share had fallen to less than one-third. Secondly, following the series of mergers from 1959 onwards, and especially in 1968, some of the large tariff companies probably decided that they were now large enough to be able to dispense with the pooling of market loss statistics for those particular classes of risk. Certainly the abandonment of the accident tariffs was opposed by some of the smaller members. The General Manager of the Friends' Provident & Century, Mr. D. B. Tregoning, was reported as saying at the 1969 conference of the Chartered Insurance Institute that:

> ". . . he was of the opinion that in these days of mergers there was developing a considerable deterioration in the amount of co-operation between companies. Certain big companies had steam-rollered over things in recent months".[10]

To turn to marine insurance, in 1884 the companies transacting marine business in London formed the Institute of London Underwriters which operates through a number of Joint Committees on which Lloyd's underwriters are represented. Amongst its many activities the Committee recommends premium rates and surcharges for certain types of risks, e.g. war and hull (fleet) risks, which are followed voluntarily by most of the London market and many foreign insurers. In addition the Technical & Clauses Committee produces sets of standard clauses for use with the basic marine policy.

Only in life business have the associations (the Life Offices' Association, the Associated Scottish Life Offices and the Industrial Life Offices' Association) refrained from regulating or recommending premium rates. The only notable restriction on competition is the L.O.A. agreement on the rates and timing of commission paid to brokers and agents.

In 1971 as a result of severe competition from companies which were not members of the Life Offices' Association, one major company, the Equity and Law, asked for the relaxation of

---

[10]   *Journal of Chartered Insurance Institute* vol. 67 (1970) p228.

14

this agreement. When its request was refused it reluctantly left the Association[11].

The trade association linking together all types of British and Commonwealth insurance companies operating in the UK is the British Insurance Association. The only possible influence this body so far has had on competition is through the advertising campaign it conducted following the collapse of the Fire Auto and Marine in 1966 and the subsequent failure of other cut-price motor insurance companies. The advertisements advised members of the public to insure only with B.I.A. member companies in order to obtain full security, and as applicants for membership needed to produce at least three years' satisfactory accounts, the advertising campaign, to the extent that it was successful, made it more difficult for new companies to enter the market. None of the companies that later failed were members of the Association until the Vehicle and General collapsed in February 1971. Then the initial unwillingness of the B.I.A. members to meet the underwriting debts of the company, apart from compulsory third party insurance bodily injury claims, largely discredited the value of Association membership in the eyes of the public[12].

One development which could have implications for the future was the establishment of a Motor Risks Statistical Bureau by the B.I.A. as recommended in a report commissioned from the management consultants McKinsey and Co. in 1965. The Bureau is now producing motor loss statistics from experience supplied by a number of member companies, including both ex-tariff and independent companies.

Entry to and exit from the industry

Like other industries, the population of firms comprising the insurance industry is constantly changing through the appearance of new entrants and the departure of existing firms through failure and amalgamation. Indeed at certain periods during its history insurance has been noted for its high failure rate. Table 1.8 records the extent of such movement over the last 90 years.

Table 1.8
Entry to and exit from the industry of British insurance companies and collecting societies

Years	Companies wound up	Companies amalgamated	Companies becoming subsidiaries	Total	New entrants	Change in numbers of independent companies
1880-89	53	56	0	109	187	76
1890-99	91	89	0	180	197	17
1900-09	65	100	16	181	253	72
1910-19	116	67	40	223	99	−124
1920-29	60	26	28	114	53	−61
1930-39	33	8	10	51	32	−19
1940-49	2	1	4	7	22	15
1950-59	9	1	15	25	29	4
1960-69	13	19	29	61	138	77

Source: *Insurance Directory and Year Book—1971*
List of companies wound up, amalgamated companies, allied companies

[11] See *Policy Holder* Insurance Journal 8 Jan. 1971 p35 & 2 Jul. 1971 p1129.
[12] See *Policy Holder* Insurance Journal 5 March 1971 p367.

Unlike many other countries, Britain until recently placed very few legal restrictions on the establishment of new insurance companies, other than the regulations relating to the formation of companies in general. The Assurance Companies Acts of 1909 and 1946 imposed certain minimum capital/solvency requirements, but otherwise (with the sole exception of industrial life business [13]) any company was free to commence insurance business in Britain. Moreover certain types of insurance business, notably liability (other than motor and employers' liability) and livestock insurances, remained outside the scope of the Acts. Such freedom to establish and transact insurance business applied equally to British registered and foreign companies.

The obstacles which a new company encounters in trying to enter the industry will be examined more fully in chapter 7, so suffice it to say here that until the late 1960's entry to the British insurance industry had been relatively easy.

This position was changed to a certain degree by the provisions of the Companies Act 1967. Now all new entrants are required to obtain authorisation from the Department of Trade and Industry in order to commence insurance business in Britain. Such authorisation is subject to [14]:

    (a) the minimum paid-up share capital of a company being not less than £100,000;

    (b) the assets of the company or society exceeding its liabilities by not less than £50,000. In the case of a foreign company transacting general business abroad its assets must exceed its liabilities by the prescribed solvency margin;

    (c) adequate reinsurance arrangements having been made;

    (d) every officer of the company or its parent company, or other person controlling the company or one-third of its voting power being a fit and proper person.

In granting an authorisation the Department may impose for a period of up to five years certain requirements relating to the provision of information to the Department, classes of investments and the maintenance (and deposit) of adequate assets in the United Kingdom.

These more stringent regulations followed a substantial rise in the number of new entrants in the 1960's (see table 1.9) and the failure in 1966 of the cut-price motor insurance company, the Fire Auto & Marine, under circumstances which led to criminal charges being brought against its principal officers.

---

[13]   In view of the special nature of its business with the poorer members of society industrial life business had attracted the attention of the legislature as early as 1875. Under the provisions of the Friendly Societies Act 1875 and the Collecting Societies & Industrial Assurance Companies Act 1896 companies transacting such business were subject to special controls regarding formation and the conduct of their business.

[14]   See sections 60-65.

Table 1.9
Entry to the UK insurance market

Year	British registered companies	Foreign companies	Total
1957	0	4	4
1958	5	8	13
1959	3	2	5
1960	6	8	14
1961	6	6	12
1962	9	9	18
1963	16	15	31
1964	19	7	26
1965	17	4	21
1966	23	4	27
1967	13	4	17
1968	16	12	28
1969	13	6	19

Source: Department of Trade & Industry.

Besides controlling new entry the new regulations also extended the supervisory powers of the Department. Broadly they provide for:

(a) extra information to be supplied by companies in their annual returns to the Department (s.71 and 74);

(b) for life funds to be valued at least every three instead of every five years (s.78);

(c) the solvency margin for general business (i.e. the amount by which the value of the assets must exceed the liabilities of the company) to be raised from 10% of general premium income to a sum computed as follows (s.62 and 79):

General premium income in last financial year	Solvency margin
Not exceeding £250,000	£50,000
£250,000—£2,500,000	20%
Over £2,500,000	Aggregate of £500,000 plus one-tenth of premium income exceeding £2,500,000.

(d) the Department to be notified of any changes in the officers or control of a company or its holding company (s.81);

(e) the Department to be given extra powers of inspection, rights to enter and search premises and to demand the production of documents if they think that there is good reason to do so (s.109-110);

Also the Department is given powers to:

(f) issue an order restricting a company from accepting new business (or renewing existing general business policies) if the Department is not satisfied that the company meets the solvency requirements, or if it fails to meet any of the requirements applicable when applying for authorisation (s.68);

(g) impose requirements of the four types applicable on granting authorisation if it appears that the business of a company is being so conducted that there is a risk of it becoming insolvent (s.80);

(h) petition for a winding-up order if a company fails to meet the above solvency requirements (s.81).

Thus the Department may hasten the exit of a company from the industry, and the reports for the first three years of operation showed that during 1967-69 sixteen investigations were made under section 109, one requirement was imposed under section 68, and 10 petitions were made for winding-up orders[15]. The failure of the Vehicle & General in 1971, however, once more raised the question whether the Department's powers are sufficiently extensive or whether it is adequately staffed to exercise its powers effectively. At the time of writing, these and other questions are still under consideration by the Tribunal appointed to inquire into the affair[16].

Brokers and agents

As noted above the practice of employing brokers and agents is a long standing feature of the insurance industry. Full-time insurance brokers have acted as intermediaries between insurer and client since the earliest days of marine insurance[17], and in 1721 the Royal Exchange Assurance appointed its first agent to obtain fire insurance business for the corporation[18].

The distinction between brokers and agents cannot be precisely defined though two main differences between them can be distinguished. First an agent is the agent of the insurer, whereas a broker is the agent of the insured who employs him to effect insurance. However, both are remunerated by the insurer by payment of commission on premiums handled, and moreover a broker may perform certain duties as agent of the insurer, e.g. issuing cover-notes and collecting premiums. Secondly, unlike an agent, a broker holds himself out to the public as possessing an expert knowledge of insurance business and the insurance market, and ought to have access to a representative range of insurers.

The membership rules of the main brokers' associations also stipulate that the placing of insurance shall be a broker's main occupation. Although evidence of experience in the business is required from applicants, only the Corporation of Insurance Brokers prescribes minimum (insurance) educational requirements.

Unlike the United States and Canada, British law does not require brokers to be officially licensed, despite representations made by the Association of Insurance Brokers to the Board of Trade during 1966 and 1967 for such legislation[19]. Consequently there is no protection afforded to the public, other than that provided by the normal laws of agency, against unqualified

---

[15] *Insurance Business* reports for 1967, 1968 and 1969. HMSO.
[16] For a description of the Insurance & Companies Dept. see R. L. Carter "The watchdog grows up" *Policy Holder* 26 July, 1968.
[17] See H. E. Raynes, *op cit.*
[18] B. Supple, *op cit*, p51.
[19] See *Brokers Chronicle* February & March 1967.

persons using the title "insurance broker"[20].

The insurance companies have appointed part-time agents from amongst a wide section of the business community including accountants, estate agents, solicitors, bank managers, garage proprietors, building societies and other persons with sufficiently wide local contacts to be able to introduce business to the companies. Although agents are unable to offer the same standard of service as a qualified broker to either insured or insurer, only in recent years have insurers introduced discriminatory commission rates, providing better terms for brokers.

A practice which increasingly has been condemned by brokers is the appointment by insurance companies of, so-called, own-case agents, i.e. the appointment of a person or firm as an agent solely for the purpose of obtaining its own business. Then the payment of commission is effectively the same as a premium reduction.

In industrial life assurance the companies use full-time "agents" to collect premiums and canvass for new business, the "agents" in fact being employees of the companies.

Apart from the firms which are members of the recognised broking associations (see table 1.1) definite numbers of brokers and agents are not available. The Economist Intelligence Unit has estimated that at the end of 1969 there were between 8,000 and 9,000 organisations calling themselves brokers but probably no more than 5,000 to 6,000 were full-time insurance inter-mediaries[21]. The membership of the associations was given as follows, the large broking groups which include several subsidiary companies being counted as one organisation:

Table 1.10
Membership of the brokers' associations at end-1969

Association	Number of member firms
Lloyd's Insurance Brokers' Association	269
Corporation of Insurance Brokers	1,571
Association of Insurance Brokers	1,050
Federation of Insurance Brokers	330
Institute of Insurance Brokers	Not available

Source: Economist Intelligence Unit *Insurance: Profile of an industry*.

The share of the market controlled by brokers varies substantially between different classes of business. As noted already, all of Lloyd's business passes through the hands of their authorised brokers. This fact alone gives brokers a major share of marine business; the Economist Intelligence Unit estimated that it could be as high as 90 per cent of total marine premium income.[22]

---

[20] On the other hand American state laws in this field have been described as being designed more to protect the agent than the public: see S. L. Kimball & B. A. Jackson "The regulation of insurance marketing" in *Essays in insurance regulations* (1966) Ann Arber.

[21] *Insurance: Profile of an Industry, op cit.*

[22] *Insurance: Profile of an Industry* p10, *op cit.*

A similar proportion of pensions business is handled by brokers, and their other main sphere of influence is in the placing of the fire and accident insurance business of industrial and commercial firms. In all of these fields expert knowledge of the market is required to achieve the best insurance arrangements relative to the needs of the insured.

Although over the last 20 years there has been a rapid growth in the numbers of suburban brokers dealing with the business of smaller firms and individuals, the overall influence of brokers in these fields remains small. A survey by the Consumer Council, for example, showed that advice had been sought from brokers by only 2 per cent of the individuals interviewed when effecting life policies, 3-4 per cent for household insurances and 22 per cent for motor insurance[23]. The life figure differs substantially from the estimate by the Economist Intelligence Unit that brokers control 29 per cent of whole life premium income but the explanation may lie in the fact that brokers tend to handle large sums assured for the higher income groups which is confirmed by the distribution of respondents in the Consumer Council sample.

The relative failure of brokers to penetrate the personal insurance market can be partly explained by the fact that the major broking firms generally regard such business as uneconomic. It is pertinent to note that the Economist Intelligence Unit calculated that 55-60 per cent of all brokered business is handled by the 23 largest incorporated (i.e. members of the CIB) brokers.

Among the potential developments in the small business end of the industry are an increase in interest by some of the large insurance companies in direct selling, and a similar growth of interest among the clearing banks in marketing insurance. The company most heavily committed to increased direct selling of insurance to the public is the Commercial Union which besides opening insurance counters in department stores is in the process of opening "office shops" in town shopping areas. The banks with their large numbers of local branches and their reputations for integrity, possess an enviable potential for the development of insurance marketing.

On the other hand the spread of suburban brokers enabled many of the new insurance companies entering the industry during the 1960's to obtain countrywide representation without the need to establish branch offices. Thus brokers reduced the barriers to new entry to the industry.

Relationships between parties

Like many other markets insurance involves three distinct parties, the producers of insurance (the insurers), intermediaries (brokers and agents), and the buyers of insurance. In practice these relationships sometimes are not so distinct as at first appears.

---

[23]   *Insurance. A Consumer Council Study* (1970).

The fact that a broker may act as agent of both the insured and the insurer has already been mentioned. In the last two years the potential conflict of interest this creates has been criticised by the Courts in *Anglo-African Merchants Ltd. and Exmouth Clothing Co. Ltd. v. Bayley* (1969) *and North and South Trust Co. v. Berkeley* (1970). Though both cases involved Lloyd's brokers the criticisms are equally applicable to all other brokers.

Possibly the dangers inherent in a broker serving two masters lay behind the decision of the Committee of Lloyd's regarding the proposed take-over in 1971 of Lloyd's brokers C. E. Heath & Co. Ltd. by the insurance company group Excess Holdings Ltd. The Committee effectively killed the take-over by announcing that a broker controlled by an insurance company would not be permitted to deal at Lloyd's.

On the other hand, many principals of Lloyd's broking firms are also underwriting members of Lloyd's, and many of the major broking firms wholly or partly own insurance companies. Although there is no evidence that this situation has operated to the detriment of the public so far [24], it does present a potential threat to the independence of advice a member of the public can expect from a broker.

A disturbing feature of most of the motor insurance companies which failed in the late 1960's, and also later of the Vehicle & General group which went into liquidation in 1971, was the ownership of broking firms by the companies themselves. Of course it may be argued that in one sense this is little different from an insurance company which deals direct with the public, and in any case is a feature of many other industries where manufacturers acquire or establish retailers to distribute their products. The essential question from a public interest standpoint, however, is whether members of the public know that they are dealing with a subsidiary or whether they are left to believe that they are receiving advice from an impartial independent firm.

The buyers of insurance

So far the buyers of insurance have not been mentioned. These range from the humblest of families to giant industrial and commercial groups and the public corporations at home and abroad.

At the top end of the premium scale it is now common practice for large organisations to operate their own insurance departments staffed by experts able to handle all insurance matters, including the negotiation of claims. This poses a real threat to the business of brokers who in some instances have found their services dispensed with except for insurances placed at Lloyd's. On the other hand a 1969 survey of over 100 medium to large industrial and commercial companies with their own full-time insurance

---

[24] See R. L. Carter, *op cit*, p228f

managers found that around 70 per cent continued to employ
brokers to place their business on the company market [25]. Many
see the insurance manager as complementing rather than replacing
the broker provided the latter is prepared to adapt to the new
situation.

It is safe to assume that no firm insures all of the risks which it
is possible to insure; all find it cheaper to carry some risks themselves, possibly making provision for unexpectedly large losses by
means of a special contingency fund. A few very large firms have
taken the final "self-insurance" step of establishing their own
insurance companies, often called captive insurance companies;
they underwrite (principally) the firm's own insurances.

This is not a particularly modern phenomenon. Imperial
Chemicals Industries Ltd., for example, owns such a subsidiary
(Imperial Chemicals Insurance Ltd.) which was established by
Nobel Industries Ltd. in 1926. Also a captive insurer is not a
substitute for conventional insurance arrangements. Initially the
underwriting capacity of a captive is limited by its paid-up capital,
and subsequent growth will be curtailed by the limited spread of
risks available to it unless it seeks to obtain business from outside
its holding group, which may involve considerable acquisition
costs. Therefore it is unlikely that the captive will ever be able to
underwrite more than a relatively small proportion of a group's
total insurance requirements.

One advantage a captive insurer gives a group is access to the
reinsurance market which may enable it to obtain forms of insurance not readily available from direct insurance companies. Also
because of a captive's own direct interest in reducing the losses of
its holding group its business will be viewed favourably by reinsurers [26].

Various reasons have been advanced for the formation of captives,
e.g. to avoid the expenses element in the premiums charged by
insurers; to share in the profitability of the group's insurance
business; to obtain insurance protection against risk not available
from conventional insurers; to increase the capacity of the market
to handle the group's business, etc [27]. Ignoring the fact that
alleged cost savings may be more illusory than real, it may be
argued that the main arguments for the establishment of captive
insurance companies rest on the shortcomings of the conventional
insurance market to meet the insurance demands of large corporations efficiently and effectively. This, of course, would be denied

[25] *The status & techniques of insurance managers in industry &
commerce*, pB25 Report of Research Group No. 3 of the Association of
Insurance Managers in Industry & Commerce (1969).
[26] J. A. S. Neave "Current Problems of the Reinsurance Market"
Policy Holder Insurance Journal 5 Feby. 1971.
[27] Inadequate market capacity, for example, was the main reason
advanced for the formation of a captive by the British Aircraft Corporation
Ltd.: see *Policy Holder* Insurance Journal 5 Feby. 1971 p192.

by the market [28] but the higher are the expenses of conventional insurers or the less effective they are in relating premiums to the loss expectancies of their insured, the greater is the incentive for a large group to seek alternative arrangement for carrying its own risks [29].

At present the number of captive companies operating in Britain is small and they control substantially less than one per cent of total non-life premium income. Nevertheless, and even allowing for the continuing dependence of their parent companies on the market for the major part of their insurance requirements, the significance of captive companies as a further extension of the countervailing power possessed by very large buyers of insurance should not be underestimated. One major insurance company, the Eagle Star, has recognised not only the problems which will be caused by an increase in the number of captive companies but also the opportunities it presents. It has helped to establish and manage several such companies for large industrial and commercial groups [30].

---

[28] See, for example, E. Orbell reported in *Policy Holder* Insurance Journal 19 February 1971 p312.
[29] See R. L. Carter "Prospects for captives" *Policy Holder* Insurance Journal 31 July 1970.
[30] See "Prospects for captives", *ibid*.

PART II
INSURANCE AND THE UK ECONOMY
Chapter 2: Risk and Insurance

Professor Frank Knight wrote in 1921 that "uncertainty is one of the fundamental facts of life" [31], and it is true that no individual or firm is free from exposure to a wide range of uncertain events which may either pass almost unnoticed or dramatically change the course of life. In everyday language it is common to refer to all uncertainties as risks, but in order to develop an understanding of the nature of such phenomena and of the way in which they may be handled, more precise definitions of uncertainty and risk have been formulated [32].

One of the first writers to attempt to distinguish between risk and uncertainty was Dr. A. H. Willett. In 1901 he defined risk in terms of an objective phenomenon capable of being measured empirically, and then used the term uncertainty to describe each individual's personal subjective evaluation of an objective risk situation [33]. Knight on the other hand distinguished two groups of uncertainties; one where probability can be calculated either on *a priori* grounds or statistically, and the other group for which only a subjective estimate of probability is possible. The first group he called risks and the second the true uncertainties [34].

Knight's definition, whilst it dealt with the objective-subjective distinction, did not make it perfectly clear whether risk should be measured by a probability value or by a measure of variation. This is a matter of some importance in relation to insurance, as will be shown, and therefore has been pursued by other writers [35].

The distinction between probability and variation in expected result may be illustrated by an example. Most owners of buildings are concerned as to whether their property will suffer damage by fire, and if so the extent of such damage. Conceivably reliable statistical data may be available showing both the frequency and severity of fires which have occurred in such buildings in recent years so that, provided conditions have not changed, the statistics may give a good guide to future expected losses. Therefore each owner will have an objective measurement of the uncertainty regarding fire loss, though in fact the information will be of very limited value to him. He may obtain from the data a probability

---

[31] F. H. Knight *Risk, uncertainty and profit* (1921) reprinted by Harper & Row (1965) p347.
[32] See, for example, *Essays in the theory of risk and insurance* edited by J. D. Hammond. Scott, Foresman & Co., Glenview, Illinois (1968).
[33] A. H. Willett *The economic theory of risk and insurance* (1901) University of Pensylvania Press 1951.
[34] *Ibid.*
[35] See, for example, David B. Houston "Risk, insurance and sampling" in *Essays in the theory of risk and insurance, op cit.*

distribution of losses of differing severity, and then calculate such statistics as the probability of suffering a loss in any one year exceeding a certain proportion of the value of his property, or his average expected loss for any one year. Yet however sophisticated the analysis may be the basic problem remains that each owner may either entirely escape having a fire or incur an actual loss varying between nil and a total loss. In other words, even with an objective measure of probability there remains uncertainty regarding the actual outcome. Therefore risk may be defined as objective doubt as to the outcome of an expected event, such doubt being measured by the degree of variation of possible results.

If this concept of risk is applied to insurance companies it can be seen that although they are dealing with the same probability situations as the individuals whose interests they insure, their degree of risk is of a different nature. By combining a large number of individual exposure units insurance companies enjoy the advantages expressed in the law of large numbers in that their actual results will more closely approximate to expected results. Thus for an insurance company expected loss becomes a more meaningful statistic, the degree of variation in actual results being inversely related to the square root of the number of units insured.

Such variations in expected results help to explain why individuals are prepared to pay premiums exceeding their average expected losses. For example, in fire insurance expenses and commission frequently comprise 40 per cent of the total premium, so that the owner of a building valued at £10,000 with an average (annual) loss expectancy of £20 will be asked to pay an annual premium of around £33.33. However, by insuring the insured substitutes the certainty of a known cost of £33.33 per annum for the risk that his actual losses in any one year may vary between nil and £10,000. Thus by insuring the individual eliminates his risk, while the insurer is able to reduce risk by grouping the experience of a large number of similar buildings.

It is this process of risk transfer, and thus of risk reduction, which constitutes the primary function of the insurance industry, and is the source of its main contribution to the welfare of society. However, in order to appreciate the full extent of the benefits provided by the availability of insurance it is necessary first to examine the nature of the costs resulting from the existence of risks and then to consider other methods of handling risks.

The cost of risks

The cost of risks to society falls under two headings. There are the losses directly caused by the occurrence of the underlying perils. In addition certain losses arise simply from the existence of risks and from the reactions of individuals thereto.

Regarding the former cause of loss, Mowbray and Blanchard point out that risks vary in their nature and distinguish between "pure" and "speculative" risk situations [36]. They classify as pure risks those situations where for an individual the actual outcome of an event can range only from a loss to at best no change in his position. If there is also the possibility of gain then the risk is of a speculative nature. Although in practice the distinction frequently is not so clear cut as this, it does draw attention to the range of possible outcomes in different risk situations and for different persons. Generally speaking pure risks form the subject-matter of insurance, whereas speculative risks, such as the risks arising from changing market situations, remain the responsibility of the entrepreneur.

The most direct form of loss caused by the operation of a peril is damage to, or other loss of, physical property and injury to persons. Such losses may be measured in economic terms by the fall in (or even total loss of) the market value of a commodity, or an individual's actual and potential earnings. Such a valuation, however, may be a very inadequate assessment of the individual's total loss. It makes no allowance for a wide range of non-economic, yet very real losses, such as the loss to an individual of the sentimental value attached to a particular article, or the pain and suffering incurred by an injured man and his family.

Frequently there ensue additional consequential losses. For example, estimates of fire losses published by the British Insurance Association make no allowance for loss of production and unemployment caused by fires. Moreover such losses embrace a wider range of economic units than the individuals and firms directly involved, extending to employees, suppliers, and customers. Ultimately society as a whole may suffer through the wastage of economic resources, and the possible adverse effects on the balance of payments.

Finally costs may be incurred in attempting to minimise the direct losses. Resources consumed in salvaging operations or the treatment of injured persons are obvious examples.

It is difficult to identify some of these losses with any degree of certainty and even more so to quantify them. For example, other firms may be able to take advantage of the misfortunes of their competitors to expand their own production and sales so that the total loss to the national product is less than the aggregate of the losses of individual firms. Similarly, laid-off workers may be able to find alternative employment. The non-economic losses are particularly difficult to evaluate; although contingencies giving rise to injury of human beings may be partially costed in terms of loss of present and future earnings, only subjective

---

[36] A. H. Mowbray & R. H. Blanchard *Insurance* (1959) p7 5th edtn. McGraw-Hill.

valuations can be attached to pain and suffering.

To turn now to the costs resulting from the mere existence of risks, these fall under two headings.

First there are the costs involved in the handling of risks. For individuals and firms this mainly involves additional expenditure on loss prevention measures, insurance and so forth, plus the time spent in deciding on the best course of action. For society the loss may be measured in terms of the benefits which would accrue from the best alternative uses of such resources, plus other resources employed by society as a whole for the control of risks, such as the police and fire services.

Secondly there is the loss of utility (satisfaction) due to the reaction of firms and individuals to risk. Some firms may be deterred from undertaking certain risky forms of production, so depriving society of goods which may yield higher levels of satisfaction than those produced in their place. Consumers, too, may prefer to forgo the satisfaction to be obtained from certain goods and services because of the risks attaching to their owner- ship and/or use.

Methods of handling risks

An individual or firm confronted by a risk has several alternative courses of action.

Risk avoidance: The most radical approach is to avoid the risk, which will involve either abandoning the proposed activity or perhaps undertaking it in a different manner. In the majority of cases risk avoidance is a practical possibility only at the planning stage of any undertaking and even then may involve considerable cost either in terms of actual expenditure or benefits forgone. Therefore other methods of handling the risk generally have to be chosen.

Risk prevention: Once the decision has been taken to accept the risk it may be possible to reduce either its probability of occurrence or the severity of the loss if it occurs. Mowbray & Blanchard[37] in dealing with such risk prevention measures subdivide them into:

> preventive: eliminating the cause of loss;
> protective or quasi-preventive: protecting things or persons exposed to damage or injury;
> minimising: to limit loss to as small a compass as possible;
> salvaging: to preserve as much as possible of the value of damaged property or the ability of injured persons.

All of these measures involve additional costs and can be justified only so long as the return (expressed as a reduction in the individual's, or firm's, loss expectancy) is as high as can be obtained from other forms of investment. Moreover complete prevention is rarely possible so that some risk will remain.

---

[37] *op cit.* p31.

Risk combination: Under certain circumstances it may be possible to reduce the risk by combining it with a large number of other exposure units. So, for example, a company operating from a large number of separate premises can reduce the risk associated with, say, the breakage of windows or the breakdown of small items of plant by centralising responsibility for all losses which occur throughout the organisation. Thus the firm will be able to predict losses with greater accuracy and make provision accordingly.

Risk assumption: The remaining risks may either be assumed by the individual or firm, or transferred to an external body. The dangers of assuming one's own risks lie in the possibility of a loss occurring which is large relative to one's financial resources. Even a smaller loss may cause severe problems if it occurs when a firm's liquidity is low and credit is difficult to obtain. The only possible safeguard is to build up a contingency fund and maintain it in highly liquid assets in order to meet any unexpectedly large loss. This, however, would necessitate higher capital ratios and lead to less efficient use of funds.

Risk transfer: The only remaining course of action is to transfer the risk. Various examples of such behaviour can be given; landlords frequently transfer responsibility for damage to their property to their tenants; under contracts of carriage often full responsibility for the safety of the goods is transferred to one or other party; and it is common practice to insert similar provisions in repairing contracts. The most important risk transfer mechanism, however, is insurance. In return for a known premium payable at the inception of the contract the insured is able to transfer to the insurer the risk of losses which may be uncertain as to both amount and time.

The value of insurance

Although not all risks are insurable [38], the insurance industry is constantly enlarging the range of risks against which it will offer protection, so that it plays an increasingly important role in the economic and social life of the country. Its value may be considered in relation to the costs and methods of handling risk discussed above.

In chapter 1 it was shown that the basic function of insurance is to provide protection for the individual, firm or other organ-

---

[38] Ideally the insurer should be able to measure the risk objectively; there should be a large number of fairly homogeneous exposure units available to the insurer; losses should be determinable and capable of measurement in money terms; and losses should be fortuitous so far as the insured is concerned and not influenced by his behaviour. Few if any of the risks which are insured measure up fully to these ideals.

isation against the financial losses which may arise from the occurrence of pure risks. Thus its main value is in minimising the costs arising out of the public's reaction to risk rather than by influencing the size of the losses which actually occur due to the operation of the perils insured. On the other hand because the insurance industry's own profitability is closely related to the latter type of losses through its claims costs, the industry has an interest in seeing them reduced.

To deal first with reaction to risk, insurance enables firms to operate with a greater degree of security, and without the need to set aside capital in highly liquid contingency funds. Exactly what this means in terms of the stimulus given to technological progress, competition and improved use of capital funds, it is impossible to say. So far as is known no research has been undertaken in this field, and it would be a difficult task because of the lack of standards against which to measure the effects of the availability of insurance. Therefore it is possible to make only the following qualitative assessment.

Even multi-plant firms, which are partially protected from catastrophic losses through the geographic spread of their assets, may incur legal liabilities beyond their resources. The claims presented against the manufacturers of the drug thalidomide are a relevant, even if fortunately rare, example. It is doubtful whether even the giant international corporations could absorb every possible loss to which they are exposed without severe financial strains. Therefore unless very large contingency funds were established, which for many small firms would need to be far larger than their present capital-employed, the population of firms would become less stable than it is with insurance. An increase in the number of bankruptcies would not be caused by any fall in business efficiency but would be the result of the random occurrence of large losses due to the operation of various perils.

It is difficult to analyse what the macro-economic effects would be of firms either requiring larger amounts of finance to maintain highly liquid contingency funds, or otherwise assuming higher levels of risk. Certainly the only other alternative would be for firms to avoid the risks of very large losses associated with the production of certain goods, which would deprive society of the satisfaction such goods provide.

If firms chose to hold large contingency funds they would encounter other difficulties. Due to the way in which the capital market (using that term in its widest sense) operates, each firm is faced with a relatively inelastic supply of finance, so that initially an increase in the capitalisation of firms would have to be met either from smaller distributions of profits or by additional long-term borrowing from the capital market at more onerous terms; the unreliability of bank credit and other short-term finance would make it unsuitable for the purpose. The negotiation of a stand-by credit may seem a possible alternative, but this probably would be offset by a reduction in the firm's borrowing capacity for other purposes. The result of these moves would be either a cut in new investment or consumer expenditure, both of which would lead eventually to an even greater fall in the level of the national income. In the longer run firms may seek to raise additional internal finance, or pay a return on the additional capital raised from the market, through higher prices. Although all firms would find themselves in a similar situation, low risk firms and those enjoying a degree of monopoly power would be more advantageously placed than others.

Any finance which firms acquired for the purpose of hoarding as contingency funds would not have the same beneficial effects on the economy as capital acquired to finance investment. It would lead to no increase in the productive capacity of the economy and generate no additional incomes. The same would apply to subsequent saving to finance the establishment of new firms; part of the money subscribed would be withdrawn from the circular flow of income instead of being returned through investment expenditure.

In order that the contingency funds would be available immediately to meet any unexpected loss, they would have to be kept in a highly liquid state secured against capital losses on realisation. This would restrict choice to bank deposits or very short-dated securities such as Treasury Bills. In effect there would be a transfer of bank deposits from households to firms. It could be argued that bank deposits covering contingency funds would be less volatile than the deposits of individuals and in due course this would enable banks to reduce their cash ratios and expand bank credit. At best this would be a long-term process, and the resultant increase in short-term credit would be unlikely to offset the extra demand for long-term capital unless accompanied by radical changes in the financing of business enterprise.

Thus it may be concluded that a wholesale substitution of contingency funds for insurance would adversely affect the economy through:

1. the less efficient use of funds;
2. a consequent lowering of the rate of economic activity;
3. a general raising of prices; and
4. a movement of resources towards lower risk and more highly monopolised industries.

The inefficient use of funds argument receives further support from the fact that insurance companies by reducing overall risk are not only able to operate safely with smaller aggregate funds, but also the bulk of their funds can be channelled back into the economy through the operations of the capital market.

The alternative possibility of firms assuming their risks without accumulating contingency funds is an equally unattractive situation. The instability this would cause has been mentioned already, and though the deleterious effect the increase in bankruptcies would have on business efficiency cannot be measured, it would be no less real. Again, the pressure would be for higher prices to compensate for the increase in risk, and once more there would follow a resource allocative effect with consumers suffering some loss of satisfaction.

Finally it may be seen that without insurance small firms in either of the above situations would be at a greater disadvantage than their larger rivals, so weakening the pressures of competition within the economy.

Influence on actual losses

To turn now to the other source of losses caused by risks, on occasions it has been argued that the existence of insurance increases the number and amount of losses which do occur. The economist J. B. Clark in speaking of fire insurers wrote,

> ". . . in view of one of their effects, they may be said to be created for the purpose of increasing the number of buildings destroyed by fire."[39]

It is well known that many crimes have been inspired by hopes of benefiting from insurance, especially in the early years of its history before the development of forensic science and laws regarding insurable interest reduced the probability of securing a profit[40].

Though today few insured may go to such lengths many still verge on the borders of dishonesty or indifference. Mark R. Greene in dealing with the American market states that,

> "Every underwriter knows that fire losses are more frequent in depression periods. During the depression of the 1930's, life insurers had such a substantial rise in the frequency of claims for disability income that the coverage had to be withdrawn almost completely."[41]

This is but one example of what underwriters term moral hazard. The authors of American insurance text-books generally distinguish between moral hazard and morale hazard. The former is treated as a condition arising from the character of the insured, who may actively seek to cause a loss or, if it occurs, either do little to limit its extent or fraudulently seek to inflate the resulting claim. Morale hazard, on the other hand, is used to

[39] "Insurance & Business Profit" in *Quarterly Journal of Economics*, vol. 7, 1892.

[40] See, for example, A. C. Campbell *Insurance & Crime* New York, G. P. Putnam's Son (1902). P. J. Stevens has stated that most cases of aircraft sabotage have been associated with attempted insurance fraud; "Fatal Aircraft Accidents", p28, *The Criminologist* Vol 4. No. 12, May 1969.

[41] *Risk & Insurance* 2nd edtn p.7 South-Western Publishing Co. (1968).

describe the attitude of many insured who, being protected by insurance, take less care to prevent loss.

Underwriters are well aware of the adverse effect of moral and morale hazard on losses and so claims, and actively seek to exercise control through selection of business, policy conditions, the investigation of claims and loss prevention surveys. Likewise discriminatory premium rates and the loss prevention activities of the insurance industry generally encourage the reduction of risk.

The complete range of loss prevention activities undertaken by British insurers is too wide to deal with here in detail, and includes financial support for many organisations involved in controlling accidents and other losses. Of particular importance, however, are the activities of insurance surveyors, who besides providing underwriters with information required to evaluate individual risks, are able to exercise some control over moral hazard and generally make recommendations for the improvement of risks. Likewise claims officials and loss adjusters appointed by insurers play an active role in reducing losses through expert advice on salvaging operations, and fire insurers maintain Salvage Corps in London, Glasgow and Liverpool which attend all major fires in their areas. Also worthy of special note is the recently established BIA Motor Repair Research Centre which is studying methods of reducing the costs of repairs.

Policy conditions are used to control such aspects of moral hazard as the regular removal of waste materials, the fencing and maintenance of machinery, etc, and by requiring the insured to carry part of his own risks. Also it may be noted that insurance rarely fully compensates a policyholder for all of the losses he will sustain by the occurrence of a risk. Willett made the point that insurance does not provide for the non-economic losses discussed earlier [42].

Discriminatory premium rates perform two functions. Firstly they avoid the cross-subsidisation of high risk groups by lower risk groups. Secondly, by penalising hazardous features of particular risks and insured with bad claims records, they provide financial encouragement for the reduction of risks [43]. Fair discrimination is difficult to achieve, however, because of the many risk factors involved in non-life insurance, the limitations on available statistics, and the continuously changing risk situation [44]. Also beyond a certain point it undermines the basic principle of insurance that the losses of the unfortunate few are paid by the many.

---

[42] op cit p12.

[43] See C. A. Williams *Price discrimination in property & liability insurance*. University of Minnesota Press (1959).

[44] See, for example, G. B. Hey "Statistics and non-life insurance" Vol. 133 Part 1, 1970, Series A (General), *Journal of the Royal Statistical Society*.

It is impossible to say exactly where the balance lies between the effects of moral hazard and the attempts by insurers to control and reduce losses. Irving Pfeffer suggests that the net effect should be a reduction in losses, but he admits that "it would be difficult to estimate the net result of the two phenomena" [45].

Few attempts have been made to study the influence of insurance on actual losses. Observation that two groups, one insured and the other not, differed in their behaviour would be inadequate proof that insurance caused more losses. For example, the fact that persons who have effected policies providing weekly benefits during disability caused by accident or sickness may suffer a higher rate of incidence and longer duration of disability than recorded losses amongst non-insured groups (measured perhaps by periods of absence from work), may well be explained as follows:

(a) the uninsured may carry on working after accidents which do not cause temporary total disablement, though at a very much impaired level of efficiency;

(b) similarly the uninsured may not be able to afford expensive prolonged medical treatment and therefore return to work earlier than is medically desirable.

Thus although the apparent loss experience of the two groups differed, the real losses caused by accident and sickness may be the same.

One detailed study of a particular class of insurance in Britain is that by Mark Hauser and Paul Burrows into unemployment insurance. Their statistical analyses did not reveal any significant increase in unemployment following increases in levels of benefit, except possibly following the introduction of earnings related benefits in 1966 [46]. It is true that these findings may not be representative of insurance in general because unemployment insurance is a very specialised area over which the insurer, the state, exercises close controls through the regulations dealing with the payment of benefits, and for the majority the lack of a job means a significant loss of income even after allowing for unemployment and supplementary benefits. Nevertheless without convincing evidence to the contrary it is reasonable to agree with Pfeffer that on balance insurance operations probably reduce rather than increase net total losses caused by the occurrence of the perils which give rise to risk.

An interesting question is whether insurers should do more in the field of loss prevention. Already some companies have entered into special arrangements for the financing of loss prevention equipment such as sprinklers, and there have been suggestions that they should make more extensive use of their

[45] *Insurance & Economic Theory* p118 *op cit.*
[46] M. M. Hauser & P. Burrows *The economics of unemployment insurance*, p104. Allan & Unwin (1969).

experience and expert loss prevention knowledge by participating in the operations of the security industry, so being able to provide their clients with a complete risk management service. American companies place considerable emphasis on the full utilisation of their highly trained engineering (i.e. loss prevention) staffs [47]. From the socialist states a Czecholoslovak spokesman recently said that in his country prevention "is regarded as one of the essential functions of the insurer, and it is a mandatory activity of both the Czech and Slovak State insurance bodies by the very legislation which governs their operations (Law No. 82/66, para. 4)" [48].

---

[47] See D. G. Vaughan *Engineering* ch. 9. in "Multiple-line insurers. Their nature & operation". Ed by G. F. Michelbacher & N. R. Roos (2nd edtn) McGraw Hill (1970).

[48] K. Urban *The economic role of insurance* p.5 of the report by the UNCTAD secretariat of the Inter-regional Seminar on Insurance and Reinsurance, Prague 20-30 Oct. 1969 published by the United Nations Conference on Trade & Development.

Chapter 3: Insurance Companies as Investors

An integral part of the business of all classes of insurance is the accumulation of substantial funds which have enabled insurance companies to become collectively the largest investors in the London capital market. Tables 3.1 and 3.2 provide a guide to the relative importance of the main institutional investors although there is a certain amount of double counting because of cross-investment between institutions, e.g. insurance companies have substantial holdings in investment trusts and vice versa. Also it should be noted that in table 3.1 insurance companies' assets are shown mainly at book values which may be as much as one quarter below market values.

Table 3.1
Total investment funds of institutional investors—1969

£ million

Insurance companies—					
Life funds	..	..	..	..	12,741
General funds	..	..	..	..	1,460
					14,201
Superannuation funds:					
public sector, including local authorities				2,932	
private sector ..	..	..	..	4,328	
					7,260
Investment trusts	..	..	..		4,902
Unit trusts	..	..	..	..	1,344
					27,707

Source: *Financial Statistics* Dec. 1970.

Notes:
1. Insurance companies' assets are at book values, except for British government securities and local authorities' securities which are included at norminal values.
   The assets of the other institutions are at market values.
2. The figures relate mainly to values at the end of 1969, except for insurance companies which take the end of accounting periods and the superannuation funds of local authorities which are at 31st March 1970.

In 1959 the Radcliffe Committee noted that the life and annuity funds were increasing by about £300 million a year, which in 1957 was equal to 19 per cent of the country's net fixed capital formation (public and private) [49]. Ten years later the net investment during 1969 in financial assets in the United Kingdom by members of the British Insurance Association and the collecting societies was £751 million for the long-term (life) funds and an additional £65 million for the general funds. This again was equal to 19 per cent of net fixed capital formation. Clearly, therefore, the

---

[49] *Report of the committee on the working of the monetary system* para. 238 Cmnd. 827, 1959.

Table 3.2

Holdings and acquisitions of assets by institutional investors 1969

£ million

	Total	Short-term	British govt securities	U.K. local authority securities	Overseas government & municipal securities	Company securities				Loans & mortgages	Land, property & ground rents	Agents balances	Other assets
						Debentures	Preference shares	Ordinary shares	Unit trust units				
(a) Holdings at end 1969													
Insurance companies	14,201	246	3,152	432	123	2,290	327	3,238	—	2,273	1,539	560	22
Pension funds:													
Public sector	1,686	—	125	53	6	189	3	828	51	251	209	—	6
Local authorities	1,246	36	243	294	6	87	7	447	116[2]	—	4	—	6
Private	4,328	95	544	146	37	667	33	2,366	721	46	311	—	11
Investment trusts	4,902	170	77	1	1	125	125	4,340	—	—	—	—	63
Unit trusts	1,344	47	18	—	—	28	21	1,229	—	—	—	—	—
(b) Net acquisitions during 1969 (cash values)													
Insurance companies	816	47	107	−20	−13	122	−4	148	—	201	186	40	2
Pension funds:													
Public sector	124	2	−36	−1	—	37	−1	84	4	−1	37	—	—
Local authorities	108	3	23	−3	—	25	—	53	2	—	—	—	5
Private	277	6	9	−1	−1	82	3	83	21	3	70	—	2
Investment Trusts	34	56	44	−1	—	23	−3	−100	—	—	—	—	15
Unit trusts	172	−1	13	—	—	—	—	159	—	—	—	—	—

Source: Financial Statistics, Central Statistical Office, December 1970 Tables 69-75.

Notes
1. Property unit trusts only
2. Local Authorities' Mutual Investment Trust and property unit trusts.
3. See notes 1 and 2 of Table 3.1.

investment policies pursued by insurance companies have a considerable influence on the efficient allocation of capital.

As can be seen from table 3.1 the life funds are almost nine times larger than the general funds. This is due to the different characteristics of the main classes of insurance business. Non-life business is essentially short-term, contracts in the main being for periods of one year or less and the bulk of the funds cover liabilities to policyholders for the unexpired periods of their policies (known as the reserves for unearned premiums) plus provisions for claims which have been reported but are still outstanding. In the normal course of events a non-life insurer can expect to have met almost all of his liabilities under insurances accepted during any one year within three or four years. The bulk of life business, on the other hand, is essentially long-term. The system of level annual premiums, often payable over 20 years or longer, means that the insurer accumulates funds during the early years of his contracts to meet the excess of claims over income in the later years when mortality rates are heavier and endowment policies begin to mature. So life funds are available for long-term investment, and indeed successful investment is essential to maintain the solvency of a life fund because an assumed rate of interest is included in the calculation of premium rates.

In addition to the funds necessary to cover their liabilities to policyholders, both life and non-life insurers endeavour to build up additional reserves to meet possible increases in claims and expenses; investment losses; and, in the case of life business, any shortfall in investment earnings. As noted in Chapter 1, authority for a company to carry on general insurance business in Britain is conditional upon it maintaining a prescribed minimum margin of solvency[50]. The larger is a company's free reserves relative to the amount of insurance business transacted, the more freedom it will possess in deciding upon its investment policy[51].

Life and annuity business is of especial importance to the economy because of its role as a medium for the collection of savings. Together with the pension funds, life insurance is a major source of long-term contractual savings, so that the investment policies of life insurers determine how a substantial part of personal saving reaches industry. L. S. Berman noted that during the 1960's pension contributions by employees plus individual premiums were on a gently rising trend, having risen from 4.0 per cent of personal disposable income in 1960-62 to 4.6 per cent in 1966-68, whereas the ratio of total personal savings had showed no upward trend over the same period[52]. He added that, "Over

[50]   See p16
[51]   For a fuller discussion of the creation and role of insurance funds see G. Clayton & W. T. Osborn *Insurance Company Investment*. G. Allen & Unwin, Ltd. (1965).
[52]   "Role of the personal sector in the flow of funds in the United Kingdom" *Economic Trends*, November 1969, Table 9, p xv.

the five year period 1964 to 1968 the net increase in these funds (life assurance and pension schemes) has accounted for nearly two thirds of total personal saving." [53].

Life office investment and the public interest

The interest of policyholders in the degree of security and the rate of return provided for their savings is only one aspect of the public interest in the investment policies of the life offices. There are wider issues. In the first instance, what effect does life insurance have on the volume of savings in the economy? Secondly, do the investment policies pursued by the life offices aid the efficient allocation of funds and thus help to stimulate economic growth? And finally what are the effects of their activities on the Government's economic policies?

In the space of this chapter definitive answers cannot be given to any of these questions. The problems they pose are difficult, by their nature defying conclusive proof, so that it is possible here to provide only a guide to the economic significance of these aspects of life insurance operations.

Life insurance and savings

As noted above, there is ample evidence regarding the relative importance of life insurance as a source of savings, but this cannot be interpreted as proof that it actually increases the overall flow of personal savings. It would be very difficult, if not impossible, to obtain valid statistical evidence on such a subject because of the many factors which influence both levels of savings and the forms they take. For example, income tax concessions undoubtedly have favoured life insurance as a method of saving, as shown by the substantial fall in single premium policies effected following the removal of income tax relief for such policies by the Finance Act, 1968.

Nevertheless it is logical to argue along theoretical lines that the availability of life insurance tends to increase rather than decrease personal savings. Firstly, the life offices together with other institutions provide an organisational framework through which savings can be made. More important, however, is the pressure brought to bear on individuals by the representatives, agents and advertising of the life offices to set aside part of their current income in order to obtain financial security against either premature death or old age [54].

There are counter-arguments along the lines developed in the previous chapter, i.e. in the absence of insurance, in order to obtain the same degree of security as is provided by life insurance

---

[53]   *Ibid* p xvi
[54]   A major weakness of the Post Office life insurance scheme instituted in 1865 and eventually closed to new entrants in 1928 was the absence of collectors to canvass for business. See D. Morrah *A history of industrial life assurance* p31 G. Allen & Unwin Ltd. (1955).

and annuity schemes, individuals would have to set aside a far higher proportion of current income to establish adequate contingency funds. This argument, however, probably is of less validity than in relation to the non-life risks of firms. Every insurance salesman knows that he has to overcome the natural reluctance of most individuals to think of old age and death and to make financial provision accordingly. Despite the efforts of the life offices apparently over half of UK households scattered through all social classes remain without whole-life insurance and a similar proportion do not possess endowment policies [55]. Although it cannot be demonstrated statistically it is doubtful whether many of the uninsured make adequate alternative provisions. Moreover once the individual has been persuaded to effect a life policy he accepts a continuing contractual obligation to save which is absent from other forms of saving apart from house-purchase and hire-purchase repayments and the recently introduced S.A.Y.E. schemes.

Therefore on balance one may conclude that the operations of the life offices increase the total flow of savings.

The contractual nature of life insurance also is of economic significance from the standpoint of the stability of the savings flow. Keynesian theory demonstrates that from a macro-economic standpoint the desirability or otherwise of a high level of saving depends upon prevailing economic conditions. Savings constitute a withdrawal from the circular flow of income so that during a period of high unemployment any increase in the public's desire to save further depresses the level of economic activity. On the other hand under demand-pull inflationary conditions increased saving has the beneficial effect of reducing the inflationary pressures.

Over most of the post-war period since 1945 Britain has enjoyed a very low rate of unemployment and economic opinion has generally been in favour of raising the level of saving relative to Gross National Product in order to provide for higher levels of investment. Thus life insurance can claim to have played a valuable role in the economy. Even in Spring 1971, with unemployment running at over 800,000, the highest figure for more than 30 years, a reduction in saving would not be an unequivocally beneficial stimulus to the economy in view of the continuing cost-push inflationary pressures.

To turn to savings in periods of economic depression, evidence shows that in the past the contractual nature of life insurance has been effective in maintaining net saving. Even in the worst years following 1929 both British and American life offices maintained a positive, though temporarily reduced, cash inflow [56]. Under such conditions the net effect of saving on the level of economic activity

[55] *Insurance*. A Consumer Council Survey. (1970) Tables 2 & 12.
[56] See G. Clayton & W. T. Osborn, *op cit*, pp 66 & 67.

depends on what happens to the net additions to savings. If they are held as cash then the full impact falls on income through a further decline in economic activity as the withdrawals effect of savings comes into play. On the other hand if savings are passed on to the capital market, given the present marginal efficiency of capital, interest rates will tend to fall so helping to stimulate investment and thereby reduce the deflationary effect of savings. In order to meet their contractual obligations to policyholders the pressures on life offices to invest funds as they accrue are such that even in a depression they are unlikely to stay out of the capital market for long. Therefore their investment policies minimise the deflationary effects of the flow of savings which come into their hands [57].

The allocation of funds

If industry operated in perfect markets where competition would eliminate inter-firm variations in profits, then differences in profits between markets for different commodities would be a reflection of differences in (a) relative supply and demand conditions and (b) the risks associated with the production of different types of goods and services. If risk is ignored and it is further assumed that there exists no divergence between private and social costs/benefits in any market, then the description by F. Lavington of an efficient capital market could be taken as correct, i.e. a market where funds are channelled to the points of highest yield [58]. Given all of the imperfections of commodity markets and the presence of risk, then yield maximisation is no longer an adequate indicator of efficient allocation of funds. The problem is to find a better measure which can be readily used to compare the behaviour of different groups of investors.

Various adjustments to such a crude measure as yield alone have been advocated. Writers such as Markovitz and Tobin, for example, have stressed the importance of investors allowing for risk in arriving at expected yield when seeking to optimise individual portfolio choice [59]. However, a statistical exercise designed to evaluate investment behaviour allowing for differences in risk would be a major study in its own right and is well beyond the scope of this book.

The same remarks apply to adjusting yields to eliminate the impact on profits of both monopoly power and other market imperfections. In any case it is arguable whether such an adjustment should be made when attempting to evaluate the degree of

---

[57] For a fuller discussion of this subject see G. Clayton & W. T. Osborn, *op cit*, pp 222f

[58] F. Lavington *The English Capital Market* p13 Methuen & Co (1921).

[59] H. M. Markovitz *Portfolio Selection: efficient diversification of investments* J. Willey & Sons Ltd. (1959) J. Tobin "Liquidity preference as behaviour toward risk", *Review of Economic Studies*, Vol. 25, February 1958.

efficiency achieved in the allocation of funds. While investors may be expected to allow for risk, it is unrealistic to suggest that investors like life offices, when selecting their investments, should discriminate against firms exploiting monopoly power to maximise profits because a life office's own survival in a competitive market depends on earning the highest possible rate of return on its funds. If it is considered that the public interest is jeopardised by firms using their market powers to earn excessive profits the remedy lies in the hands of the state, not with investors. Therefore, in looking at the investment behaviour of life offices the discussion here will proceed on a largely qualitative basis concentrating on attitudes to yield and risk.

Like other investors life offices in determining their investment policies have to pay regard to a number of external and internal constraints. Portfolio choice is limited by such factors as the size and quality of local capital markets, tax regulations, other government regulations and the nature of their own contractual obligations. Some of these constraints are specific to life offices, others are of more general application. Analysis by a number of writers [60] of the determinants of the portfolio choice of life offices has laid stress on their primary need to minimise yield risk (i.e. the risk that the rate of return on their funds may fall short of the interest rate assumed in calculating premiums) and has emphasised the need to maximise expected yield, including prospective capital gains. At the same time the long-term nature of their liabilities, the stability of premium income and the consistently positive cash inflow of growing life funds make the need for liquidity, and consequently capital-certainty, of minimal importance (it may be added that in the UK the practice of valuing assets and liabilities on the same basis minimises the effect of fluctuations in market values for the purposes of statutory solvency requirements). This list of internal constraints is by no means exhaustive but it will suffice for present purposes.

One may deduce from the above that life offices are long-term investors, who in attempting to maximise yield are able to invest part of their funds in securities which are not readily marketable but, as noted by the Radcliffe Committee, life offices do have "a broad bias in favour of matching liabilities with securities" [61] as a protection against yield risk. In addition a high proportion of the contracts issued by most life offices are on with-profit terms where liabilities are not wholly fixed at inception and in an era of inflation policyholders expect protection in real as opposed to solely money terms. Therefore, one may expect ordinary shares and

[60] See, for example, G. Clayton and W. T. Osborn, *op cit*; L. D. Jones *Investment policies of life companies* Harvard University Press (1968). G. M. Dickinson *Determinants of insurance company asset choice* Withdean Paper no.2. Withdean Publications Ltd. (1971).
[61] *Op cit*, para. 244.

other equity type investments, which in the past have provided some hedge against inflation, to be attractive assets for some part of life funds. Finally the size of the funds at their disposal permits life offices, without incurring disproportionately high transaction costs, to pursue policies of portfolio diversification in order to minimise the risk of the overall yield on the fund deviating substantially from the expected return.

These hypotheses can be tested by analysing the actual investment behaviour of the life offices but no empirical data is available to test any theory of how life policyholders would invest their savings in the absence of insurance. Therefore any conclusions regarding the net effect of life offices on the allocation of funds must be reached on purely deductive grounds.

The act of effecting life insurance indicates that in relation to death the individual is risk-averse, preferring to forgo current income in order to obtain financial security for himself and/or his dependants. Basic life insurance contracts guarantee that a specified sum will be available as planned. If it is assumed that in the absence of insurance the individual retained the same attitude to risk, then liquidity and capital-certainty would be of paramount importance in investing savings. Few forms of investment could meet such requirements. As argued in chapter 2 regarding non-life contingency funds, the individual would be restricted in his choice to savings bank, building society and finance house deposits, and short-dated securities.

Perhaps the individual would be prepared to accept some trade-off of security in order to secure higher yield but unless the assumption regarding attitude to risk is substantially relaxed long-term investment would be out of the question. Securities which are not readily marketable, such as the shares of unquoted companies, would be totally ineligible as a form of investment.

Thus it may be concluded that life offices are less risk-averse in their investment policies than would be the individuals who provide them with their flow of funds. The result is to increase the volume of funds coming to the long-term capital market, with the emphasis being placed on allocating funds to firms able to provide the highest expected yields. To the extent that policyholders do have differing attitudes to risk, the supply of with-profit and equity-linked policies to those prepared to accept some risk in order to achieve a higher expected yield enables the life offices themselves to invest in riskier equity-type securities.

Other aspects of savings being channelled through institutions such as life offices are that skilled investment analysis should improve efficiency in the allocation of funds, and concentrating large funds in the hands of a single investor makes possible forms of investment which could not otherwise be undertaken given the present organisational framework of the economy. For example, the life offices provide house purchase and business mortgage loans, finance property development, and provide sale and leaseback finance, operations which it would be difficult for small savers to undertake. Likewise together with other institutional investors, life offices are able to improve the working of the new issue market, reducing cost and risk, by accepting placings of the smaller new issues and acting as underwriters for public issues of shares and loan stock.

One other issue raised by Professor G. Clayton and W. T. Osborn is whether the life offices by acting as long-term speculators could have a greater stabilising influence on the stock exchange where short term speculation predominates [62]. They made the point that at the time of writing life offices appeared to act as long-term investors, buying to hold, rather than as dealers in securities. Statistics now available of quarterly acquisitions and sales of securities (published in *Financial Statistics*) challenge that view, and discussions with investment managers indicate that a growing number of offices are becoming ever more active in managing their portfolios. Also, as will be discussed later, net acquisitions of different classes of security show that the life offices respond to changing investment opportunities from year to year. It is true that many small offices still have to rely on "two men and a boy" [63], so virtually precluding investments of a type calling for lengthy investigation and/or considerable specialist knowledge, but with adequate access to stock broker and other information services, in general the quality of investment expertise appears to be improving.

It would be rash to conclude from the foregoing that more could not be done to improve the influence of life office operations on efficient resource allocation. Evidence shows that in general, for reasons of risk, administrative costs, and difficulties of investigation and portfolio management, life offices do not provide finance for innovators and new firms. Also their investments in very small firms not only comprise less than 1 per cent of their total invested funds, but also such investments are restricted to mortgage loans and sale and leaseback arrangements [64]. A case could be made from the stand point of the public interest for more finance to be provided for all of these areas of economic activity. However, it is not clear that the life offices would thereby improve their own investment performance, nor that they would be acting in the strict economic interests of the nation. Though, for example, it may be desirable from a social standpoint to provide more finance for small firms it is doubtful whether there are many *efficient* credit-worthy small firms who deserve more finance but

---

[62] *Op cit* p233f.
[63] *Op cit* p 235.
[64] See p115 "*Financial facilities for small firms*, a study by Economists Advisory Group directed by Dennis Lees. Research report no 4 of the Committee of Inquiry on Small Firms, HMSO (1971).

are unable to obtain it at present from one or other of the many sources available [65].

Government economic policy

To speak of government economic policy as if it related to some given set of objectives, always mutually compatible and unchanging over time is a travesty of the truth. Basic objectives change in the light of developing economic, social and political conditions and philosophies; different policies are employed to achieve those ends; and in the medium term the priorities attached to different objectives may alter, e.g. full employment becoming subordinated to an improvement in the balance of payments. Moreover economic policy is only one part of the overall objectives of governments which may place greater emphasis on social or other objectives than on purely economic ends; for example, it may be considered preferable to accept a rate of economic growth lower than that which is attainable in order to achieve a balanced distribution of industry, and thus employment, throughout the country, or to reduce the pollution of the environment.

Therefore, the operations of a particular sector of the economy in relation to government economic policy cannot be evaluated simply in terms of efficient resource allocation. If instead it is assumed (perhaps unrealistically so) that the public interest lies in all sectors of the economy conforming to the economic policies of the government of the day, then an examination of the behaviour of any particular set of institutions can proceed along either of the following lines. The theoretical approach would be to ascertain whether particular institutions (here the life offices) could possibly operate counter to the policy methods selected by the government to achieve its objectives. The alternative approach would be to study their actual performance over the years relative to contemporary government policies. The influence of life insurance on the flow of savings has been discussed already so the following remarks will be confined to investment policies.

The conventional economic weapons at the disposal of governments can be classified broadly as fiscal, monetary and physical. The last by means of direct controls such as building licences, import quotas, etc. can affect the relative profitability of different industries and thus unavoidably influence the investment opportunities and yields available to investors. Fiscal policy likewise influences business profitability, and may vary the net of tax return on different classes of investments, so over time changing their relative attractions to investors; e.g. the imposition of capital gains tax made growth stocks and fixed-interest loan stock issued below par relatively less attractive than previously. Such policies act as constraints on the behaviour of all types of firms and in so

---

[65] *ibid*, p70.

far as their interests are adversely affected by governmental action they may be expected to attempt to minimise the effects thereof; conversely incentives which are in accord with their own objectives should meet with a favourable response. The life offices in determining their investment policies find themselves in the same position.

Although the offices may be powerless through their investments to counter the effects of fiscal and physical policies on overall and relative levels of profitability in industry, so long as the maximisation of expected yield remains their primary investment objective the government may expect them to respond to such changes in deciding their investment policies. Thus government measures designed either to reduce aggregate demand, or to control demand in certain sectors of the economy, may be expected to encourage life offices to seek alternative areas for the investment of their funds because of the curtailment of profits and thus expected yields in private industry. On the other hand relaxations of controls and fiscal stimuli may fail to produce a desired flow of funds from life offices if the improvement in yield is regarded as being of temporary duration.

The main area where life office investment behaviour may conflict with government policy, however, is in relation to monetary policy. As noted above, the life offices are major financial institutions forming an important part of the capital market, and as the Radcliffe Committee observed, a firm unable to obtain credit from one source usually turns to another institution [66]. This demonstrates the importance of Bank of England directives being applied equally to all financial institutions and not merely the banks. Although in the 1950's dissatisfied bank customers may have been able to obtain longer-dated loans from life offices, today the insurance industry is asked to abide by the same qualitative requests as the banks. Also from time to time specific requests have been addressed to the industry, such as the constraints on lending for property development during the mid-60's. In so far as the life offices adhere to such requests their investment behaviour will be consistent with government policy. So long as control is based on moral suasion alone it must be recognised, however, that scope for conflict remains, particularly when Bank of England requests do not appear to be consistent with the offices' own yield-maximisation objectives.

Generally it has been assumed that institutions like the life offices have no influence on effective monetary demand in that they merely act as intermediaries passing on the loanable funds created by the savings of their policyholders. Clayton and Osborn argued, however, that such a view would have to be modified if analysis of life offices' investment behaviour "revealed that there

---

[66] *op cit*, para 125, p42.

were significant variations in the rate at which they transmitted funds to the various outlets for investment" [67].

They concluded that the offices' attitude to liquidity for pre-cautionary and speculative motives is so weak that they do not contribute "to the instability of monetary demand by absorbing and releasing cash", but they may increase effective demand by lending for capital formation "the proceeds from the sale of assets, particularly Government securities, out of their existing port-folios" [68]. If such sales of existing securities are taken up by the monetary authorities or by the public out of spare money balances, then the life offices are able to place at the disposal of borrowers a volume of credit which is in excess of their current flow of funds from policyholders and investment income. Lack of empirical evidence prevented Clayton and Osborn from proceeding beyond the point of recognising the possibility that life offices may act in such a destabilising way at a time when the monetary authorities are seeking to control the money supply by restraining the banks and allowing interest rates to rise.

Today more statistical evidence is available. The published statistics of the flows of funds show that in each of the years 1963 to 1969 inclusive the insurance companies maintained positive net acquisitions of British government securities, though in 1966 they fell to a very low ebb (see table 3.3).

Table 3.3
Net acquisitions of assets by life assurance funds with considerable business in this country

	1963	1964	1965	1966	1967	1968	1969
Cash and short-term assets	I	16	−5	−15	26	−7	35
British government stocks	110	92	57	28	219	127	120
U.K. local authority securities	25	—	24	−2	3	15	−20
Overseas government etc. securities	2	−2	−4	−4	3	−2	−11
Company securities:							
Fixed interest	167	197	210	217	147	179	103
Ordinary shares	119	142	72	85	61	189	131
Loans and mortgages	93	129	179	161	92	145	192
Land, property and ground rents	60	57	93	117	104	126	183
TOTAL (excluding changes in agents' balances etc.)	577	630	624	588	654	773	733

Source: The financial institutions: Part I, Table C, Bank of England *Quarterly Bulletin*, Vol. 10, no. 4, December 1970.

This, however, does not prove that the life offices consistently support government policy; the figures may simply reflect the attractiveness of high fixed interest, (default) risk-free securities in

[67] *op cit*, p226.
[68] *op cit*, p227.

an era of economic uncertainty. Support for this view is provided by the fact that in every year, apart from 1969, gilt-edged acquisitions varied inversely to acquisitions of debentures, no doubt reflecting in part the availability of new debenture issues.

Moreover quarterly details of net acquisitions present a somewhat different picture from table 3.3, revealing wider swings in investment behaviour. In one quarter of each year, except 1963, 1964 and 1967, sales and redemptions exceeded acquisitions of British government securities. According to data published in *Financial Statistics*, the largest net sales of gilt-edged securities occurred as follows:

1966—1st quarter	£24·0 million net sales			
1968—4th quarter	£10·4	,,	,,	,,
1969—1st quarter	£2·8	,,	,,	,,
1970—2nd quarter	£15·3	,,	,,	,,

An examination of the economic conditions prevailing in each of the above periods lends support to Clayton and Osborn's argument that the operations of the life offices could exert a destabilising influence on money demand. All four quarters were marked by grave doubts as to the state and future of the British economy, leading to heavy market selling of gilt-edged securities at times when the government was seeking to limit domestic credit-expansion. In 1968-69 the authorities largely allowed the market to find a new level, with gilt-edged prices consequently falling and yields rising, but in 1966 and 1970 they made substantial purchases of gilt-edged securities in order to stabilise interest rates. In each period the life offices contributed to the sales of gilt-edged securities while adding to their holdings of company securities.

In 1966 the selling of gilt-edged securities was prompted by the deterioration in the balance of payments and the political uncertainties prior to the announcement in March of the general election. These factors coincided with large debenture and equity issues, the latter after a long period in which new issues had been small. The response of the life offices was to sell medium dated (5-15 years) gilt-edged securities and increase their net acquisitions of debentures, ordinary shares and mortgages.

The fourth quarter of 1968 and the first of 1969 can be treated as a single period. Again the balance of payments, inflation and general doubts as to the country's economic recovery following the 1967 devaluation, which led to further deflationary measures in November 1968, produced heavy market selling of gilt-edged securities. During the fourth quarter of 1968 the life offices used the proceeds of their sales to build up their short-term assets, and to provide more mortgage loans, possibly in response to demand for credit by companies and from private house purchasers. In 1969 the life offices modestly increased their holdings of undated gilt-edged stocks but their main swing was towards debentures in response to large new issues and a widening of the yield relative to gilts. The high proportion of convertible debentures amongst the new issues gave investors in 1969 an opportunity to take advantage of the prevailing high fixed-interest rates, yet at the same time make provision to switch to growth stocks in the future at advantageous prices, so giving further incentive to switch funds from gilts to debentures.

Lastly, in the second quarter of 1970 there was growing concern regarding inflation at a time of economic stagnation, rising unemployment, industrial unrest and an approaching general election. This triggered off substantial selling of long-dated government securities and a slump in equity prices, the F.T.-Actuaries Ordinary Share Index dropping almost 20 per cent during April and May. The life offices joined in the sale of long-dated gilt-edged stocks, at the same time taking advantage of the lower prices to acquire equities, although new issues were at a low level.

Consequently although the life offices undoubtedly acted in the immediate interests of their policyholders, taking advantage of investment opportunities as they arose, the implications of their actions from the standpoint of government monetary policy possibly were less beneficial.

Investment practice in the 1960's

Today, insurance companies when questioned invariably claim to have the same investment objectives of maximising the expected yield on both life and general funds, yet their investment portfolios reveal a wide diversity in the policies actually pursued. For example, expressing the balance sheet values of the main categories of investments as a percentage of total invested assets, the 1968 life accounts of British companies revealed the following very wide range of variation between companies:

Table 3.4
Distribution of life office investments, 1968
% of total investments (book values)

	(unweighted)	(weighted by size of fund)	Minimum	Maximum
British government securities ..	17·0	16·5	0	63
Debentures ..	16·4	18·5	0	43
Ordinary shares ..	25·4	24·6	0	74
Property and rents	8·4	11·5	0	81
Mortgages	18·4	17·2	0	85

Source: "Life Office Investments" *Policy*, vol. 68, no. 3173, December 1969.

Such differences may be explained by dissimilarities in the liabilities of the companies; different attitudes to risk; divergent views regarding expected future performance of particular sources of investment; etc. It does mean, however, that the following description of the investment policies pursued by the insurance market as a whole must not be interpreted as being typical of any one single company.

The growth and distribution of insurance funds during the late 1950's and the 1960's is recorded in table 3.5. However, the figures must be interpreted with a good degree of caution because of the dispensations granted to insurance companies regarding the valuation of their investments for balance sheet purposes. It will be noted, however, that holdings of all classes of investments have grown over the period covered, but by far the largest increases (both absolutely and relatively) have been in equity type investments by both the life and general funds. Amongst fixed-interest securities, holdings of government stocks have shown the largest relative fall, while debentures, preference shares and mortgages collectively amount to roughly the same proportion of total holdings as in 1957.

After a substantial build-up of equity holdings in the 1950's and early 1960's, during the latter part of the period most offices tended to maintain a fairly constant ratio of two to one between purchases of fixed-interest and equity-type investments (see table 3.3). In 1968 and 1969 equity-type investments, however, comprised over 40 per cent of net acquisitions, and undoubtedly a high proportion of the new loan stocks acquired were convertible debentures which will enable the offices further to increase the equity share of their portfolios at a later date. This trend may continue with the growing popularity of equity-linked life insurance schemes, and the desire of the life offices to protect with-profit policyholders against inflation, so enabling them to retain their own competitive position in the market for personal savings.

It may be argued that ordinary shares are a less suitable form of investment for the general funds which need a higher degree of liquidity as a protection against the occurrence of catastrophe losses[69], yet the movement of the general funds away from gilts into ordinary shares is even more pronounced than for the life funds. The reasons are not difficult to find. The tax saving provided by franked investment income relief on equity dividends is particularly important for general business which is dependent upon investment income for profits, and in an inflationary era it is essential that the companies build up their reserves to match their increased liabilities. So long as premium income continues to grow liquidity is of limited importance and non-life insurers appear to make provision for it by maintaining a higher proportion of their assets in cash and short-term assets[70]. Also they may restrict

---

[69] For a discussion of asset choice for general funds see C. J. Baker "Investment problems of non-life funds" *Journal* of Chartered Insurance Institute vol. 57, 1960. and G. M. Dickinson, *op cit.*

[70] In 1969 these items amounted to 9 per cent of general funds against 1 per cent of life funds: see Table D, p 425, Bank of England *Quarterly Bulletin*, December 1970.

Table 3.5
The distribution of insurance invested funds

	Life funds					General funds				
	1957		1969		Growth index 1957–1969 (1957=100)	1957		1969		Growth index 1957–1969 (1957=100)
	£m.	%	£m.	%		£m.	%	£m.	%	
1. British government authority securities	1,054	25·1	2,063	17·0	196	162	17·1	199	8·9	123
2. Foreign & Commonwealth government provincial & municipal stocks	146	3·5	371	3·1	254	297	31·4	425	19·1	143
3. Debentures, loan stocks preference & guaranteed stocks & shares	918	21·8	2,313	19·1	252	217	22·9	465	20·0	214
4. Ordinary stocks & shares	738	17·6	3,266	27·0	443	148	15·6	779	35·1	526
5. Mortgages	652	15·5	2,097	17·3	322	37	3·9	114	5·9	308
6. Real property & ground rents	397	9·4	1,503	12·4	379	45	4·8	162	7·3	360
7. Other investments	298	7·1	501	4·1	168	41	4·3	83	3·7	202
	4,203	100·0	12,114	100·0	288	947	100·0	2,227	100·0	235

Source: British Insurance Association

Notes:
1. All assets shown at balance sheet values.
2. In 1969 British government authority securities includes all investments issued by public or local authorities or nationalised industries in the U.K. which previously were included in the category of "other investments".
3. The figures are not strictly comparable with table 3.2, the B.I.A. statistics including the investments of Commonwealth companies operating in the U.K.

their equity purchases to the more stable stocks with active markets.

Some life offices, such as the Norwich Union, have for many years invested a relatively high proportion of their funds in property but during the second half of the 1960's there was an all-round upsurge of interest in property as a class of investment by both life offices and other institutions. Partly this reflected the general demand for equity investment at a time when new issues of ordinary shares fell after the introduction of corporation tax, so that there was a danger of institutional investors bidding up the prices of ordinary shares. Undoubtedly it also was influenced both by the growing uncertainty in security markets in the face of inflation, and, at a time when bank borrowing was restricted, by an increase in demand from firms for finance which could be met by liquidating fixed assets through sale and leaseback arrangements. The demand from business firms for long-term credit may also partly explain the buoyancy of mortgage loans during the period, though the high levels of interest rates and the provisions for changes in line with prevailing market rates no doubt encouraged some life offices to meet such demand.

Property was only one of the newer sources of investment explored by insurance companies in the 1960's, sometimes by direct investment and in other cases in association with property development companies. Some of the major companies acquired interests in such new forms of investment as equipment leasing and factoring. Others sought to increase their American investments without incurring the dollar premium penalty by entering into back-to-back loans with American companies exchanging sterling for dollars. At least two offices have tried to overcome the difficulties of providing finance to small firms by entering into arrangements with other institutions, one with a merchant bank (an experiment which failed) and the other with management consultants. It would seem that similar links with merchant banks, etc, and an expansion of the range of financial facilities provided, will become an increasingly more important aspect of investment practice in the 1970's.

Finally it must be recognised that the size of the funds at the disposal of the major offices poses its own problems. Not only does it inhibit the active management of their investment portfolios but it also raises other difficulties.

Traditionally insurance companies have avoided taking an interest in the management of the companies in which they invest for various reasons, including the fact that they have neither the time nor the staff required for such work. This desire to avoid involvement in the affairs of other companies has been helped by the limits insurers have placed on equity holdings in order to minimise risk; normally the maximum holding in any one company is fixed at 5 per cent, or at most 10 per cent, of its issued share capital. However the need to invest larger funds, with a consequent increase in the size of individual holdings, especially in smaller companies, makes it more difficult to avoid intervening if a firm's performance deteriorates, and some insurance managements are changing their attitudes to this problem. In 1969 one General Manager was reported as saying that,

> ". . . he wished he could visualise an increasing tendency for the investment manager to have an effective say in the control of the policies of companies in which insurers invested. It was not a sinister thought. Surely he had a duty to be vigilant in watching over policyholders' and shareholders' investments".[71]

Almost two years later the chairman of the Prudential spoke as follows of the way in which his company saw their role in this field:

> "Our primary function in respect of Ordinary share investments is to protect the interests of our own policyholders and shareholders. It can reasonably be argued therefore that, if we have doubts about a company's management, the proper reaction should be to sell our holding, but in our case this is unlikely to be possible. Holdings of the size which are typical of our portfolio cannot be easily disposed of at acceptable prices particularly where doubts have arisen about the adequacy of existing management. The fact that we are often one of the largest shareholders in a company therefore makes it inevitable that we will be involved in many difficult situations requiring intervention by shareholders. Our involvement in the past has usually arisen in this way and such occasions have been much more frequent than the relatively few instances which have become a matter of public comment. Indeed I would stress our conviction that problems of this nature often lead to delicate and difficult negotiations, which will have a better chance of success if they can be conducted discreetly.
> "Though we have in the past always recognised the desirability of vigilance on the part of shareholders, we have had cause to be apprehensive about political reaction to any strong display of influence exercised over companies in which we have holdings. But during the last few years a different consensus appears to have emerged that it would be in the best interests of the country if institutional investors were more vigorous in their efforts to maintain efficient management in the companies in which they invest. This could also be in the best interests of our own policyholders and shareholders and we accept that in practice the brunt of the increased effort must be borne by the large institutions such as ourselves. At the same time we believe that many advocates of more active intervention underestimate the difficulties met with in this field. We do not regard ourselves, and neither should others, as having any particular expertise in the management of industrial companies. Nevertheless, we are increasing our capacity to undertake and maintain closer relationships with companies in which we invest. In this way we should acquire a better understanding of the problems of company management."[72]

---

[71] E. Orbell, *Journal of the Chartered Insurance Institute*, vol 67 (1970) p215.
[72] Extract from the Prudential's Annual Report & Statement of Accounts for year ended 31 December 1970, p9.

In the United States fear of financial trusts has been one of the reasons why many of the states have imposed restrictions on the size of individual holdings in companies, and as the Prudential chairman implied, there have been critics in this country. Foremost amongst these has been Professor Richard Titmuss who has argued that the concentration of personal savings in the hands of insurance companies and pension funds will lead to a socially undesirable allocation of resources[73]. He saw their investment criteria as overlooking the areas of greatest social need, and social policies being "imposed without democratic discussion; without consideration of the moral consequences which may result from them"[74]. By implication he saw intervention by insurance companies in the management of companies in which they invest as a further dangerous concentration of economic power into few hands[75].

Clayton and Osborn, after their detailed study of the investment behaviour of insurers, came to the conclusion that they had not used their power irresponsibly[76]. Nevertheless the increase in insurance funds, and therefore probably in the size of individual holdings too, has been of such magnitude since 1957 that such fears cannot be brushed aside as being misconceived or of no importance. In certain respects Titmuss' arguments merit further consideration, especially in relation to the need for more investment in such necessary items of social capital as lower class housing for rental, hospitals and schools. This, however, is one of the defects of the overall economic and political system rather than something which can be rectified by tinkering with the investment criteria of institutions such as insurance companies and pension funds, although society has it in its powers to exercise more control over the investment policies of insurers. The dichotomy is whether life offices should be judged in terms of the returns they make to their policyholders, or whether they are to be set wider, non-economic objectives.

Likewise the arguments for and against intervention do not point to any simple clear-cut answer. A failure by the institutions to exercise any control over the large companies in which they invest would leave their management effectively free from intervention by shareholders to improve performance so long as an acceptable rate of dividend was maintained. Intervention on the other hand presents a danger to the public interest arising from the concentration of economic power; if the holdings of the institutions continue to grow and they actively seek to exercise their powers, then present controls over monopolies could become quite ineffective.

---

[73] "The irresponsible society" in *Essays on the Welfare State*. 2nd edtn. Allen & Unwin (1958).
[74] p216 *ibid*.
[75] p240.
[76] *op cit*. Chapters VIII & X.

It is difficult to see where the balance of the public interest lies. On the one hand only institutions such as insurance companies can restore the balance between management and shareholders in major companies so helping to stimulate efficiency; on the other hand there are the obvious dangers. Any solution would of necessity involve fundamental changes in the law relating to the complex inter-relationships between the interest of the management of companies, their shareholders, employees, customers and the public at large in a modern, developed economy.

Finally, returning to the general question of investment behaviour, although it is undoubtedly true that the insurance companies decide upon their individual investment policies in the light of both general investment criteria and their own particular attitudes and needs, the changes they make probably are often as much a reaction to events as the result of deliberate choice. On the other hand, it must not be forgotten that by their own actions and attitudes such large investors often are able to influence events. Earlier, for example, it was noted that the large-scale buying of equities and debentures in 1966 was in response to prevailing economic conditions and large new issues becoming available, but it is equally reasonable to attribute the surge in new issues at least in part to the anticipated receptiveness of institutional investors, including insurance companies, at that time.

It is difficult to disentangle cause and effect in such a field as investment behaviour. However, an approach to investment which is substantially grounded in a response to events is quite understandable in an area of decision-taking where the results of one's own actions are so uncertain, and furthermore will be substantially influenced by the decisions of other investors with a large army of competing professional investors forever pitting research against more research.

Given the difficulties of predicting the future performance of different assets, which will be dependent upon the complex inter-action of numerous factors, it is inevitable that some investors will react to changing conditions by seizing opportunities for investment in assets which at that moment in the light of prevailing conditions appear to offer the highest expected yield, even though an uncertain change in conditions soon could substantially alter yield expectations. In this process many investors are likely to be swayed by current expert market opinion so that a follow-my-leader approach to investment is observable in the markets. Expressing these thoughts in another way, in an efficient market where all investors have access to the same information it is only logical that they should reach the same conclusions regarding investment opportunities, even if their subsequent actions may differ in the light of their individual needs and attitudes to risk, and that those conclusions will be influenced significantly by circumstances beyond their control. The difficulties institutional investors face in trying to "beat the index" have been neatly summarised in the random walk hypothesis and the accompanying statistical studies [7], so that a decision merely to follow the market would not be unreasonable.

Therefore in the foregoing analysis of investment practice it may have been more correct to have interpreted some of the investment changes which have taken place as the result of circumstances largely beyond the control of insurers than as the result of deliberate choice on their part. Regrettably it is impossible to say exactly where the dividing line should be drawn.

---

[7] See Eugene F. Fama "Random walks in stock market prices" *Financial Analysts Journal*, Sept—Oct 1965, and A. C. Rayner and J. M. D. Little *Higgledy Piggledy Growth Again*, Blackwell (1966),

Chapter 4: Insurance and the balance of payments

Brief reference was made in Chapter 1 to both the overseas business of British insurance companies and the interest of foreign companies in the British market. In this chapter it is proposed to study more fully the role of the insurance industry as an earner of foreign currency, which is the third aspect of its importance to the UK economy.

Reference to foreign currency earnings should not be thought of as relating solely to receipts and payments of foreign currency during a particular period. Such transfers would give a very inadequate and inaccurate guide to the industry's contribution to the country's balance of payments, which may be defined as covering all transactions giving rise to international credits or debts. The distinction is particularly important in relation to insurance operations where the time-lag between foreign currency being earned and remittances being made to the UK may spread over many years. Often overseas earnings are invested abroad and though this gives rise to no currency flow the UK will have acquired title to foreign assets so that as the result of the transactions the international credits of the UK will have increased. Conversely remittances of overseas earnings are not the sole source of currency transfers; for example, premiums are received from, and claims payments are made to, foreigners for overseas insurances placed on the London market; changes in investment policies may result in transfers in either direction; remittances may be made abroad to strengthen reserves in particular countries; and insurers are involved in long-term capital movements whenever they invest their funds through overseas capital markets.

The resulting complexities of the currency flows, and the difficulties involved in accurately calculating the operating profits of insurance companies in any period, make the measurement of the net contribution of the industry to the balance of payments an extremely difficult task.

Some 20 years ago Professor S. J. Lengyel attempted an analysis of international insurance transactions but had cause to comment:

> "It sounds strange, and yet it is true, that the insurance business, itself based on statistical experience, in many countries lacks proper statistics about the state and development of its own affairs. Either no statistics are available at all or else they are very defective."[78]

Ten years later the United Nations Conference on Trade and Development (UNCTAD) commissioned the Economist Intelligence Unit Ltd. to prepare a report on insurance costs in the balance of payments of developing countries, but again lack of

---

[78] *International insurance transactions* p17 Wadley & Ginn (1953)

statistical data proved an insuperable problem[79]. Therefore it is impossible here to provide precise comparisons between the overseas performance of British insurers and their foreign counterparts; the best that can be achieved is to present available UK statistics supplemented by what little other data is available.

The development and future of overseas business

Insurance business essentially is concerned with spreading risks as widely as possible, and early in the 19th century British insurance companies began to establish agencies on the Continent. Professor Supple records that in 1826 the Special Fire Committee of the Royal Exchange Assurance undertook an investigation of foreign insurances following the establishment of a few agencies by the Corporation in Belgium, Holland and Germany at the end of the Napoleonic Wars[80]. In his history of the Sun Insurance Office P. G. M. Dickson mentions that although the Sun did not appoint its first foreign agents until 1836, the Phoenix had established an agency in New York as early as 1805, though it was withdrawn shortly afterwards[81]. As the century progressed the companies, and especially vigorous newcomers like the Royal and Commercial Union, followed in the wake of British merchants, establishing agencies and branches throughout the major trading areas of the world, so that by the end of the century the United States alone accounted for "at least 40 per cent" of total fire premiums[82].

The era of rapid expansion of overseas business continued up to the outbreak of the First World War with British insurance companies establishing agencies and branches wherever Britain made its influence felt. Such overseas business offered British insurers scope not only for a wider geographical spread of risks, with a consequent improvement in the stability of underwriting results, but also opportunities for more rapid expansion of their business than otherwise would have been possible in view of the increasing competition at home. At the same time they could offer their British clients an insurance service abroad.

The War markedly changed the course of economic affairs, disrupting old trading patterns and ushering in an era of trade restriction from which insurance did not escape. Professor Lengyel commented in 1953 that:

> "In the past half-century, and in particular since the great turning point of the First War, a narrower and pernicious nationalism has manifested itself in all facts of public life. It is now stronger than it

[79] Published by UNCTAD (1964) ref. E/CONF. 46/5. In 1965 UNCTAD proposed to study insurance, including the adoption of uniform criteria for the production of statistics by all countries.
[80] B. Supple *The Royal Exchange Assurance*, p 155 and 156.
[81] P. G. M. Dickson *The Sun Insurance Office* 1710-1960 Oxford University Press (1960).
[82] B. Supple, *ibid*, p213.

has ever been, and impinges more consciously upon every aspect of international relations. Local insurance companies, nurtured and protected by national sentiments sprout up everywhere, and with growing financial strength, experience and technical maturity they progressively displace foreign companies hitherto dominant in the field". [83]

As early as the 19th century State insurance offices were established in a number of European and other countries, but it was not until the 20th century that British insurance companies found themselves totally excluded from transacting business in an ever-growing number of countries, and subject to severely discriminatory restrictions in many others. After the 1917 revolution Russia created a precedent by the nationalisation of its insurance industry, which other countries have since followed, some, like India, paying compensation, others such as Burma making no recompense to foreign companies.

Apart from political doctrinaire causes, the reasons for economic nationalism in relation to insurance business are not difficult to find. In discussing the attitudes of developing countries the Economist Intelligence Unit listed four basic reasons why steps may be taken to exclude foreign insurance companies from their markets:

(a) The need to rationalize a chaotically fragmented market (and to stamp out malpractices sometimes associated with this situation); and to make supervision of the market easier.

(b) As national economic consciousness has grown, to encourage and develop an indigenous insurance industry and the skills associated with it.

(c) To ensure that more of the funds generated by the insurance process are retained in the country, and to control their employment.

(d) To save foreign exchange as heavy net deficits have been incurred on over-all external accounts. [84]

Sometimes it has also been believed that premiums charged in underdeveloped countries have been excessively high, while the transfer abroad of the resulting profits has created a double strain on their economies.

Besides the saving of foreign exchange and greater control over investment funds which the development of an indigenous insurance industry provides for a country, one other economic attraction is the relatively low opportunity cost involved. The bulk of the necessary capital funds remain free for investment within the country, and though the expulsion of foreign insurers may possibly mean losing the services of highly trained expatriate staffs there are usually a sufficient number of trained nationals capable of filling the key positions in the industry, which at the same time will continue to provide employment for existing local

---

[83] *op cit*, p7.
[84] Economist Intelligence Unit report, *op cit* p17.

insurance staffs. Also the existence of a highly competitive international reinsurance market eliminates the initial problem of limited underwriting capacity.

It must be emphasised that developing countries are not alone in imposing restrictions; many are only following the practices of developed nations. Even where the desire is simply to protect the interests of domestic policyholders without directly discriminating against foreign insurers, the implementation of deposit and similar regulations which restrict the free movement of funds tends to curb the activities of foreign insurers.

Under these conditions, even though those countries which pursue the most nationalistic policies continue to need reinsurance from the international markets (although often on a reduced scale), the scope for direct underwriting by British companies is contracting. Sometimes the replacement of an agency or branch organisation by locally established subsidiaries including local interests has helped the companies to retain a share of some overseas markets but for the foreseeable future it seems inevitable that the share of British companies in the markets of many developing countries must continue to decline.

This trend is supported by the policy of the United Nations which seeks to encourage and assist developing countries to establish and foster the growth of their own indigenous insurance offices. At the first Conference of UNCTAD in 1964 it was recommended that:

> "The developed countries should give their full co-operation to the developing countries to encourage and strengthen their national insurance and reinsurance markets, and should give their support to all reasonable measures which are directed to this end and to increase their retention capacity." [85]

The British delegation agreed subject to a reservation regarding the need for insurance and reinsurance to be on a fully international basis. At the second conference in 1968 it was further recommended that the insurers and reinsurers of developed countries should, amongst other things:

(a) provide insurance and reinsurance facilities to developing countries at lowest possible costs:
(b) help with research into insurance problems; and
(c) help with the training of their insurance staffs.

On the other hand if Britain is successful in its application to enter the European Economic Community British insurance companies will share in the freedoms of "establishment" and "services" proposed by the Treaty of Rome. Although draft Establishment and Service Directives prepared by a Commission of the EEC provide for the insurers of third countries to carry on business in any of its member countries, more favourable con-

---

[85] Paragraph 1, recommendation A.IV.23 of the 1st Conference of UNCTAD, 1964.

ditions are proposed for companies established in a member country so that British insurance companies would gain by Britain's entry. There are, however, risks associated with entry too; the draft directives are generally restrictive in their nature, reflecting the character of current legislation in France and Germany whose companies, unlike the British, have been confined mainly to domestic markets. Therefore, the one fear of the British insurance industry is that through the eventual harmonisation of insurance supervisory regulations in the EEC it will find itself subject to far more restrictions which may adversely affect its extensive international operations outside the boundaries of the Community, and harm the international character of the London market[86].

The extent of the industry's overseas business

Overseas business is of interest not only to the insurance companies which have established agencies, branches and subsidiaries abroad. London is the world's major international insurance market, with a unique institution in Lloyd's which, like the companies, obtains more than two-thirds of its non-marine business from foreign markets, much of it in the form of reinsurance business. Similarly the companies receive a substantial amount of reinsurance business from abroad and a certain amount of direct business, though this latter so-called "home-foreign" business is curtailed by the actions of many countries in imposing on their nationals exchange control and other restrictions to limit the placing of insurance with insurers outside their own country.

Marine business is essentially international in character. For example, the premiums for insurances effected on goods sold under c.i.f. contracts are indirectly paid by the importer in the price of the goods. In attempting to measure the relative importance of overseas business it is difficult, therefore, to obtain an accurate estimate of the premiums paid by foreigners.

Like so many other aspects of the insurance industry the exact extent of overseas premium income in the portfolios of British insurers is not known. The new regulations issued under the Companies Act 1967 require companies to show UK and overseas premium income separately in the annual returns to the Department of Trade and Industry[87], but until all of the returns for financial years commencing 1st January 1969 are published it is possible to provide only the following details published by the British Insurance Association.

---

[86] For example, see M. H. R. King "British insurance and the Common Market" *Policy*, vol 70. no 3190, May 1971.

[87] Schedule 2, Part V, General Business Premium Analysis. The Insurance Companies (Accounts & Forms) Regulations 1968, Statutory Instrument 1968, no 1408.

Table 4.1

**The geographical distribution of the premium income of members
of the British Insurance Association**

Net Premium Income 1969 £m.

	United Kingdom	United States	Rest of the world	Total (world-wide)
Fire and Accident (non-motor)	384	290	379	1,053
Motor	213	179	241	633
Marine, Aviation and Transport		181		181[88]
Ordinary long-term	958	—	202	1,160
Industrial long-term	286	—	—	286
	1,841	650	822	3,313

Source: *Insurance Facts & Figures* 1969,
British Insurance Association.

To a certain degree the table overstates the position in that the members of the B.I.A. include Commonwealth companies with offices in the UK. On the other hand certain British companies are even more highly dependent upon overseas business than these figures suggest; for example, both the Royal and the Commercial Union obtain around 80 per cent of their fire and accident premium income from abroad.

The overseas premium income of British companies is even more highly concentrated than UK business. The Committee on Invisible Exports of the British National Exports Council noted that in 1963 the four leading companies—the Prudential, Legal & General, Standard Life, and the Norwich Union Life— accounted for more than three-quarters of the overseas premium income of UK life companies[89]. Similarly in 1965 four composite groups— the Royal, General Accident, Commercial Union and the Northern & Employers (now part of the Commercial Union Group)—accounted for over two-thirds of the general insurance premiums earned by British companies in the United States[90].

Regarding Lloyd's the Committee stated:

> "Under the existing system of accounting and recording employed at Lloyd's, it is not possible to produce actual premium income figures relating to all overseas business. However, figures are available to show that U.S. and Canadian dollar business has for a considerable period of time represented approximately 50 per cent of Lloyd's total premium income, and it is reasonable to estimate that other foreign business accounts for a further 25 per cent."[91]

---

[88] It is not possible to split marine, aviation and transport business geographically as the business is transacted on an international basis.

[89] The Report of the Committee on Invisible Exports *Britain's invisible earnings,* para 217, p145, British National Export Council (1967).

[90] *ibid,* para, 218, p146.

[91] *ibid,* para. 223, p147.

On the basis of the 1968 premium income Lloyd's overseas premiums, therefore, would amount to almost £500 million, so giving an aggregate overseas premium income for all British insurers of around £2,000 million.

In addition to the companies and Lloyd's, large broking firms also have an active interest in overseas business. Brokers handle all of the overseas business placed at Lloyd's, and in 1967 research revealed that at the summit of the broking market were "some 50 firms controlling annual premium incomes of £10 million upwards and all active in overseas business, some having offices and/or subsidiary companies abroad."[92] Since 1967 mergers between major broking firms have reduced the above number (in 1971 the Economist Intelligence Unit reported that the 23 largest incorporated brokers accounted for 55-60 per cent of all brokered business)[93], but the general picture of broker participation in overseas business remains unchanged.

The contribution to the balance of payments

Overseas premium incomes should not be confused with the industry's contribution to the UK balance of payments; in order to arrive at the latter figure account also must be taken of claims payments, expenses payable abroad, overseas investment earnings, taxation, etc. Also, to obtain an estimate of the industry's net foreign currency earnings allowance must be made, too, for the overseas earnings of brokers and the UK earnings of foreign insurers.

Despite the long-standing importance of insurance in Britain's invisible exports, it is only in recent years, largely as the result of the work of the Committee on Invisible Exports, that detailed estimates have been published of the industry's foreign currency earnings. Professor Lengyel could only find "vague references to the country's net income from this source" and added that:

> "In 1947, the then Chancellor of the Exchequer mentioned an amount of £20 millions, two years later the British Insurance Association widely publicised an estimate of £33 millions. Since that time sterling has been devalued and the premium income of British insurers in terms of sterling has increased by 50 per cent. On the same, wholly inadequate, basis as that of the B.I.A. the balance should be at present £50 millions."[94]

At last more detailed information has been made available in the official annual publication the *U.K. Balance of Payments* from which table 4.2 is obtained. The overseas earnings of the industry

---

[92] R. L. Carter, *Competition in the British fire and accident market*, op cit, p224.

[93] Economist Intelligence Unit Ltd. *Insurance profile of an industry* p10, published by the Corporation of Insurance Brokers (1971).

[94] op cit, p23.

fall under four main headings:

1. operating profits (i.e. underwriting results and investment earnings) of the overseas branches and subsidiaries of British companies;
2. underwriting profits on overseas direct and reinsurance business placed on the London market;
3. interest and dividends received on portfolios of overseas securities held by UK based companies;
4. the profits of the overseas offices and subsidiaries of UK brokers, and commissions earned on other foreign business placed on the London market.

Lloyd's earnings fall mainly under category 2 plus investment earnings on funds held abroad.

Table 4.2
Net Overseas Income of the United Kingdom Insurance Industry
£ million

	1965	1966	1967	1968	1969	1970
Companies (marine, aviation and cargo business and direct and portfolio investment income)	46	66	78	90	111	111
Lloyd's (underwriting and interest	14[1]	20[1]	45[1]	74[1]	105[1]	121[2]
Brokers	21	23	27	35	41	49
UK net insurance income overseas including portfolio income	81	109	150	199	257	281
UK net insurance income overseas excluding portfolio income	50	78	115	161	214	237

[1] Three year average. [2] Two year average.

Source: UK Balance of Payments 1971
Annex 5 Table 53.

The details for table 4.2 are supplied to the government by the British Insurance Association, the Corporation of Lloyd's and the Corporation of Insurance Brokers. Although they are the best estimates available it is important to recognise that they are only estimates, for reasons which have been mentioned already. The figures, for example, do not cover the net earnings of home-foreign business (other than marine and aviation), though they are believed to be small.

It is essential to note, too, that apart from reinsurance transactions involving UK insurers the estimates do not allow for the UK earnings of overseas companies. At present these are believed to be small in relation to the overseas earnings of UK insurers but probably they are growing in view of the numbers of new entrants (see chapter 1). Moreover the increasing size of industrial and commercial risks is bound to cause a larger flow of insurance business across national boundaries, and in order to know how the performance of British insurers compares with their foreign competitors it will be necessary to obtain details of the latter's earnings in the UK.

In the *Report of the Committee on Invisible Exports* the 1965 estimate of the companies' overseas earnings was further broken down as follows: [95]

	£ million
Overseas branches, subsidiaries & agencies	19
Marine & other "home-foreign" business	2
Head Office overseas portfolio investment income	25

The extent to which it is possible to interpret the overseas results summarised in table 4.2 is limited without even more information. For example, without details regarding the additional shareholders' funds necessary to finance their overseas business it is impossible to comment on whether it is in the interests of insurers to continue to underwrite business abroad, or whether the capital employed could be used more profitably for alternative purposes. To ask such a question is entirely legitimate during an era of very low profitability in the insurance industry throughout the world, and when some companies have decided on their own volition to withdraw from the American and other markets because of the losses they have incurred.

Likewise it would be useful to have a breakdown between operating results (i.e. underwriting results plus investment earnings on unexpired premium reserves and outstanding claims) and investment earnings attributable to shareholders' funds. Underwriting results inevitably are subject to wide fluctuations due to the occurrence of catastrophes, and part of the improvement in companies' earnings over the period covered by table 4.2 is due to the disastrous impact of hurricane "Betsy" on American results in 1965. Throughout the period, however, underwriting results the world over have suffered from a combination of competition and inflation so that in many countries underwriters have had to rely on investment income for their profits. For example, the aggregate American results of the ten leading British composite companies given in table 4.3 show underwriting losses for all of the years covered.

Table 4.3
Results of the ten leading British companies in the United States of America (US reserve basis)

Year	Premiums written $000	Statutory Underwriting Profit $000		Investment income $000
1965	971,316	−46,850	−4·8	61,644
1966	1,038,866	−17,321	−1·7	69,172
1967	1,065,681	−11,067	−1·0	74,213
1968	1,111,899	−39,802	−3·6	74,308
1969 (provisional)	1,179,358	−34,704	−2·9	84,460

Source: "Top Ten in 1969" Table 4
Policy Holder Insurance Journal
9 Oct. 1970.

[95] *op cit*, para. 231, p149.

One other factor which disturbed the results was the devaluation of the £ in November 1967 which inflated the values expressed in sterling.

The data from table 4.2 is re-presented in semi-log scale form in figure 4a to show the changing rates of growth of overseas

Figure 4a
Net overseas income of the UK's insurance industry

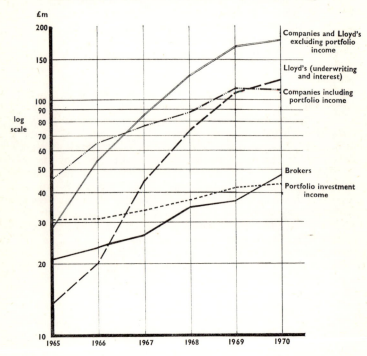

income. In addition the income of the companies and Lloyd's excluding portfolio investment income is shown. It can be seen that though income from almost all sources has increased each year the rates of growth have tended to slow down and in fact the overseas income of the companies (including portfolio income) was the same in 1970 as in 1969. On the other hand, as insurers throughout the world readjust premium rates to take account of the impact of inflation on claims costs further improvements in earnings can be expected. Moreover the industry's 474 per cent increase in net overseas income (excluding portfolio income) from £50 millions in 1965 to £237 millions in 1970 represents a major achievement by any standard, especially when it is recognised that in 1970 its contribution to the country's total invisible earnings of £540 millions was larger than those of the rest of the City put together.

In view of the above it may seem unkind to end this chapter on a discordant note, but in relation to its overseas business the industry has one cause for concern other than the implementation of further restrictive measures by overseas governments. In their paper to the 1968 annual conference of the Chartered Insurance Institute J. Plymen and S. Pullan referred to the apparent greater success of American companies in reducing expense ratios over the period 1956-1966, and the relatively poor performance of British companies on the Canadian market compared with their Canadian and American competitors [96]. The later annual surveys of composite insurers prepared by stockbrokers W. Greenwell & Co. confirm this position. Clearly if British companies are to continue their North American operations measures must be taken to improve their profitability, and it is notable that both the Royal and the Commercial Union have taken steps in this direction.

Mention has already been made of the interest of foreign insurers in the UK market, and again the British companies need to be on their mettle. During the debate on the papers dealing with insurance company mergers presented to the 1969 conference of the Chartered Insurance Institute one speaker remarked that, "Already two of the big American groups were just waiting to pounce on the British market when underwriting returned to profit". [97] Perhaps this overstates the threat but over the last decade a large number of American banks have entered the London market, and there is no reason to believe that the insurance market is not equally exposed to American competition.

[96] "Insurance Profitability, past, present & future" Journal of Chartered Insurance Institute, vol 66 (1969).
[97] R. I. Clews "Summary of discussion" p220 Journal of Chartered Insurance Institute, vol. 67 (1970).

PART III
ECONOMICS AND INSURANCE MANAGEMENT: ANALYSIS FOR DECISION-TAKING

Chapter 5: The Nature of an Insurer's Costs

Whatever the industry, successful management involves more than simply producing a commodity. Even such admirable qualities as technical excellence, innovation or high standards of service cannot by themselves guarantee business success—this was brutally demonstrated by the failure of Rolls Royce in 1971. Any firm wishing to improve its profit performance must also seek to gain an understanding of the nature of its costs and exercise effective control over them, and economic theory and concepts can be of help in this process of cost analysis.

The concept of opportunity cost

A fundamental characteristic of a firm is that it commands the use of certain productive resources which it employs to produce goods or services for sale. Thus a firm must decide how best to use the resources at its disposal in order to achieve its desired objective. Orthodox economic theory assumes that the principal objective of firms is to maximise profits, but, as will be explained in chapter 7, alternative theories have been developed recognising that firms may choose other ends, though perhaps subject to the need to earn a certain minimum level of profit in order to satisfy shareholders and keep the firm in business. The corollary of any profit objective or constraint is the need to pay regard to costs.

The present organisation and type of business carried on by a firm, and many of the resources available to it, are the result of past management decisions which at the time will have involved the firm in the expenditure of some part of its financial resources; e.g. the ownership of its business premises. This tends to lead to a common, but serious, management error of allowing present decisions to be determined by costs incurred in the past.

Economics lays stress on the fact that bygones are always bygones. Once funds have been used to purchase an asset, frequently they are irretrievably sunk in that asset. Taking an example from the previous chapter, over many years an insurance company may have expended considerable sums in establishing a network of branches in an overseas country, but now a substantial persistent deterioration in its operating results may force the company to consider whether it should continue to operate in that country or employ its resources elsewhere. In order to make a correct decision in such circumstances the type of information required is not a detailed account of past expenditure but the costs it will unavoidably incur if it stays.

Obviously future costs will include such items as claims costs, commissions to agents, staff salaries, lighting, heating, the rental of leased premises and any other items involving an actual cash expenditure. There is also the question, however, of how to treat the cost of resources owned by the company—its buildings, office equipment and vehicles—and here the use of historic costs may lead to a wrong decision. What matters is the present value of those resources to the company if employed in their best alternative use; this is the economic concept of opportunity cost, which may be defined as cost measured in terms of alternatives foregone.

So in calculating the estimated cost of continuing to underwrite business in the country under consideration, the company should impute a cost for the buildings it owns based not on their purchase price but on their present market rental values, which may be significantly more or less than original purchase price or current book values. Likewise in dealing with office furniture and equipment, vehicles, etc., original purchase price is irrelevant; the correct figure would be based on present realisable value, though allowance would need to be made for estimated maintenance costs. Moreover the time period under review has a bearing on the problem because if the company was deciding upon its long-term position then it would need to allow for the cost of replacing such assets, whereas in reviewing the position for the next year or so the question of replacement does not arise. In the short-run so long as revenue at least covers variable costs (i.e. those costs which vary directly with the amount of business transacted) then it may pay the company to remain in business.

One other aspect of reviewing costs on an opportunity cost basis, which is of considerable importance in relation to insurers, is the dual role of insurance operations. When commenting in public on their non-life business insurers generally emphasise underwriting results and tend to ignore investment earnings. This overlooks the fact that a substantial part of their investment earnings are obtained from the funds representing unearned premium reserves and provisions for outstanding claims, both of which are generated by premiums. Therefore decisions bearing on the amount of business a company is prepared to underwrite, and so on its costs, must also take account of the effect thereon of this secondary source of income.

Before leaving opportunity cost one further point deserves mention. The example used cited a company forced by poor results to reconsider its position; ideally a company should regularly re-examine all of its operations in the light of the alternative opportunities available to it. In this way it will obtain early warning of changing conditions and can begin any necessary process of readjustment long before it is forced into the situation where sudden drastic changes have to be made. On the other hand it must be admitted that the job of identifying and evaluating opportunity costs itself may involve substantial costs—management time spent in planning cannot be used for the task of getting on with the business in hand! Also it may be argued that a particular class of business, or area of operation, cannot be reviewed in isolation, because a decision regarding that business could have a significant impact on other operations of the company. So a composite insurance company may rightly decide that part of the opportunity cost of ceasing to operate in a particular country (or ceasing to underwrite a particular class of insurance) would be the loss of other business as the result of some clients transferring their insurances to other companies capable of meeting all of their insurance needs.

AN ANALYSIS OF INSURERS' COSTS

Many business decisions have to be taken on the strength of far from perfect knowledge of all of the factors involved, but at least it is possible for a firm to obtain from an analysis of its own internal records a substantial amount of information regarding the nature and behaviour of its costs.

The determinants of an insurer's costs

Broadly an insurer's costs fall under three headings:
  (i) expenses of acquiring its business;
  (ii) expenses of administering the business and dealing with claims; and
  (iii) claims payments.

The first two categories are more or less common to every type of business, and may be labelled as sales and production costs, though in insurance the product is a service rather than a physical good. It is possible for an insurer to exercise a considerable degree of control over the composition and size of such costs relative to the amount of business transacted, cost being a function of: (a) the prices paid for the use of resources; and (b) how efficiently the resources are used.

Economic theory draws the distinction between technical and economic efficiency. The former is concerned only with minimising the numbers of units of different factors used to produce a given output; so, for example, if it were possible to produce a desired output in several different ways using two factors of production, the results may be as follows:

Table 5.1
Technically efficient methods of production
Units employed

Method	Labour	Capital
1	10	12
2	7	15
3	9	12
4	7	13

Methods 1 and 2 would be rejected as being technically in-efficient because in both cases it is possible to produce the same output by another method using less of one factor without using more of another. It would be impossible, however, to choose between methods 3 and 4 without knowing the prices of the two factors. This introduces the concept of economic efficiency which is concerned with producing a given output at the least cost. Using the same example, it is possible to see from table 5.2 how changing factor prices alter total costs and point to desirable changes in production methods. In situation A the more labour intensive

Table 5.2
Factor prices and economic efficiency

	Factor prices per unit		Total cost	
	Labour	Capital	Method 3	Method 4
	£	£	£	£
Situation A	20	45	720	725
Situation B	25	45	765	760
Situation C	20	40	660	660

method of production 3 is the least costly way of producing the desired output, but when the price of labour rises to £25 per unit in situation B not only do total costs rise but also a firm would find it cheaper to switch from production method 3 to method 4. Only in situation C would a firm be indifferent as to which method it used, the fall in the price of capital compared with situation A having made the more capital-intensive method equally efficient.

This simple example illustrates the important economic principle of substitution, which states that, given a set of techni-cally feasible methods of producing a given output, efficient pro-duction involves substituting cheaper factors for more expensive ones. If factor prices change then it will tend to be worthwhile to use more of the now relatively cheaper factor and less of the relatively dearer one.

Applying this principle to insurance operations, which tradi-tionally have been very labour-intensive with perhaps 65 per cent of total management expenses being absorbed by salaries and other labour costs, rising salaries clearly have helped to speed up the use of computers in the industry; i.e. the industry has tended to become more capital-intensive. Likewise rising prices provide an insurance company with a cost incentive for relying more heavily upon brokers than upon the expansion of its branch organisation in order to achieve a growth of premium income. With agents' commissions payable on the basis of a fixed percentage of premiums collected, so long as existing commission rates can be maintained unchanged an insurer is able to minimise the effect of rising prices on costs by substituting brokers' services for its own branch organisation.

Turning to item (iii), claims payments, these do not fit into the conventional concept of a cost, not being a payment for the use of resources by the insurer. Thinking of an insurer as undertaking the function of pooling the contributions of individuals into a fund from which the claims of those who suffer loss are paid, claims payments may be conceived as being of the same nature as the transactions of the banks when repaying deposits, i.e. the discharging of liabilities to customers which thereby reduce both assets and liabilities.

This view of claims payments is particularly relevant to many types of life insurance where premiums collected over a long period are used to build up a fund from which the maturity values of the policies will be paid. Nevertheless, especially in the case of non-life insurance it is conducive to better management to think of claims as part of total operating costs, being expenditure which will necessarily be incurred in the conduct of the business. Moreover like other costs they are amenable to a certain degree of control by an efficient management.

The first step in the control of claims costs lies in the selection of the risks to be insured, which is a purely technical process depending upon the skill of the underwriter and which lies outside the scope of this book.

Having acquired a portfolio of business the resulting claims cost still remains partially within the insurer's control. As noted in chapter 2, in certain classes of insurance the insurer can exercise some influence over both the frequency and size of losses giving rise to claims, e.g. the loss prevention work of fire, burglary and engineering surveyors. Finally, after a loss has occurred the insurer's claims officials may be able to limit the size of the loss, through, for example, the expert advice provided by fire loss adjusters for dealing with salvage, or the supervision of repair costs by qualified motor engineers.

However, loss control activities themselves involve insurers in additional costs, and this is further reason for regarding claims as a cost subject to the same principle of substitution (both as between types of business and methods of dealing with claims) as other costs. Lastly it is possible for an insurer also to control its claims costs, and in particular fluctuations in total claims costs, by purchasing reinsurance. In return for a premium the reinsurer accepts an agreed part of the risk underwritten by the direct insurer, so that a known cost, the reinsurance premium, is substituted for an uncertain claims cost.

Cost uncertainty

One of the problems an insurance company faces is that at the time it sells its product it will have incurred only a small part of its potential costs; the major element, claims, will arise during the subsequent period of insurance, so that there is an element of uncertainty regarding the final total cost. It would be easy to fall into the error of regarding the insurance business as unique in this respect, and to exaggerate the degree of uncertainty involved. Firms in other industries which enter into fixed-price contracts to supply goods at a future date, e.g. shipbuilders, aircraft manufacturers and civil engineering contractors, or which tend to fix prices for long periods ahead for reasons of competition, likewise have to accept the risk that actual costs may vary from the estimates on which the price was based because of the occurrence of random or other factors affecting costs. Moreover, whilst it is impossible to predict the outcome on any individual policy, the essence of insurance is that by combining a large number of like units the insurer reduces risk, and by using past results as a guide an insurer can predict with an acceptable degree of certainty the overall result of a particular class of business.

On the other hand certain classes of insurance are particularly exposed to substantial random fluctuations in results due to the occurrence of catastrophes, e.g. windstorm insurance in hurricane zones or the insurance of jumbo jets, while others are subject to significant increases in claims costs beyond the levels indicated by past experience due to changes in risk factors which affect either the frequency and/or average cost of losses, e.g. motor business. In the last few years the accelerating rate of inflation throughout the world has been a particular problem for non-life insurance.

The difficulty with inflation is that premiums generally are fixed at the inception of the period of insurance whereas claims arise throughout the period. Consequently in the case of insurance contracts providing an indemnity where claims are settled at the prices prevailing at the time of loss, the average cost of losses will be rising throughout the period of insurance. Moreover if on average there is a long period of delay between the dates when claims arise and when they are settled, as in the case of liability and marine hull insurances, claims costs may be further inflated if the losses are paid on the level of prices applying at the date of settlement. Similarly in a period of inflation any management expenses incurred after the inception of the insurance will be exposed to the effects of inflation, So, for example, if it is assumed that for a particular class of insurance:

(i) the rate of inflation (r) affecting both claims costs and expenses is steady at 10 per cent per annum;

(ii) policies are for periods of insurance of 12 months;

(iii) claims are distributed evenly throughout the year, and are subject to an average delay (calculated by amount of settlement) of two years between the dates of occurrence and settlement;

(iv) expenses, excluding commissions and expenses paid at inception, are closely related to the dates of claims settlement; and

(v) claims and the associated expenses (C) are planned to account for 75 per cent of total costs.

Then the average time-lag (t) between the beginning of the periods of insurance and the final settlement dates of the claims arising during the period will be $0.5+2.0=2.5$ years. Therefore, with inflation steady at 10 per cent per annum, insurers' total actual costs will be 20.2 per cent above what they would have been in the absence of inflation; using the symbols above this figure is calculated as follows:

$$\text{Percentage increase in costs} = C[(1 + r)^t - 1]$$
$$= 75 [(1 + 0.10)^{2.5} - 1]$$
$$= 20.22$$

In other industries where firms enter into contracts to be completed at a future date so that costs are exposed to inflation, it is common practice to include a price adjustment clause in the contract. Unless insurers adopted a similar practice for their non-life premiums, and probably it would be difficult to do so in dealing with ordinary members of the public, the only way to protect their results from the ravages of inflation would be to load the premium at the outset for estimated inflation. In the above example, and assuming commission to be 15 per cent of the gross premium, it would be necessary to increase the premium by approximately 24 per cent, i.e.:

$$20.22 \times \left(\frac{1}{1-15} \right) = 23.8.$$

In practice the problem is not quite so simple. The first difficulty is to predict the correct rate of inflation—or possibly different rates for the various elements of claims costs and expenses—and if it was accelerating or decelerating, or if claims were subject to marked seasonal variation, then the formula would need to be adapted accordingly. If the inflation factor was being applied for the first time then further allowance would need to be made for the delay between the time of the decision to revise premiums and when, on average, that decision became effective. Also no allowance has been made for the fact that during the period between the occurrence and the settlement of claims the insurance funds will be earning interest which itself may rise during a period of inflation. Finally there is the task of persuading competitors that an upward adjustment of premium rates is required.

Apart from the special problem of inflation, the general problem of uncertainty regarding future claims costs attributable to the inevitable delay in identifying changing risk factors, and the residual risks in a portfolio due to the limited number of units included, undoubtedly does have a bearing on competitive behaviour. This subject will be discussed more fully in Chapter 7.

Fixed, and variable costs

So far, apart from mentioning different sources of costs, i.e. claims, commissions and management expenses, no attempt has been made to analyse their behaviour relative to changes in the volume of business transacted. Such analysis is, however, of fundamental importance for price/output decisions.

In the short-run the ability of a firm to vary its output is constrained by limitations on the resources at its disposal; while it may be possible to alter the numbers of some resources (e.g. unskilled labour, stationery, etc.), other factors of production, such as office accommodation, require a much longer period in which to effect any change. Thus it is conventional to divide resources in the short-run into fixed and variable factors, and these in turn lead to the division of total costs into fixed and variable costs.

A fixed cost may be defined as any cost which does not vary with output; whatever the level of output in the short run, such costs remain unchanged. Often they are referred to as overheads. A variable cost is one which varies directly with output (rising and falling with output) and in total they represent the direct cost involved in producing any desired output.

Applying these concepts to the business of an insurer, variable costs include:

(i) commissions paid to agents for business they introduce;
(ii) claims payments;
(iii) part of management expenses.

The division of management expenses between fixed and variable costs depends in part on management policy; for example, overtime earnings obviously are a variable cost but the treatment of basic salaries depends on the extent to which an insurer (a) would be prepared to lay off employees if premium income fell, and (b) could quickly obtain new suitably qualified staff. In the case of most insurance companies the type of staff required probably makes labour not very variable in either direction, although the reorganisation of working methods in some offices to enable more of the work to be undertaken by routine clerks may tend to change the position. On the other hand some management expenses undoubtedly are fixed costs (e.g. office accommodation costs) whereas others are variable costs (e.g. stationery).

The distribution of costs between fixed and variable can also be altered by the method of operation employed. Reference has been made already to the use of brokers and computers; an organisation geared to dealing through brokers with few branch offices would have a higher proportion of variable costs than a company with a large branch organisation. Conversely the replacement of lowgrade staff by the use of computers would increase the fixed cost element, unless computer time could be bought from a centre allowing considerable flexibility in the amount of time purchased.

Altogether the variable cost items form a high proportion of an insurers' total costs. The actual proportion will vary from one class of insurance to another, and also between insurers for the reasons stated above. Taking, for example, all classes of fire and accident insurance, the aggregate 1969 results of 65 British companies showed the following breakdown of costs [98]:

	Percentage of net premium income
Claims paid and outstanding, and contributions to fire brigades	65·0
Commission	15·8
Expenses and overseas taxes	19·2

Treating only one-fifth of "Expenses" as variable would produce a total variable cost figure of around 85 per cent. Excluding claims, variable costs would still amount to over half of the aggregate commission and expense costs [99].

This relationship between fixed and variable costs is of considerable practical importance. Other things being equal, the higher the proportion of fixed costs to total costs the nearer a firm must operate to its planned capacity in order to cover total costs. This can be shown by means of two break-even charts.

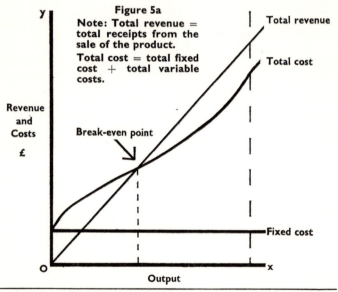

Figure 5a

Note: Total revenue = total receipts from the sale of the product.

Total cost = total fixed cost + total variable costs.

[98] "Fire and Accident Business in 1969" *Policy Holder* Insurance Journal 27 November 1970.
[99] C. Arthur Williams suggested that for American companies some 80 per cent of total non-life costs were variable. *Price discrimination in property and liability insurance.* p11. University of Minnesota (1959).

Figure 5b

**Note: Total revenue = total receipts from the sale of the product.
Total cost = total fixed cost + total variable cost.**

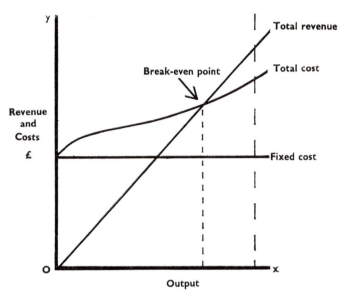

Figures 5a and 5b represent two different firms: it is assumed that all of the following factors are identical for each firm:

    (i) the planned capacity level of output;
    (ii) total costs at the capacity output;
    (iii) the product's market price, which remains unchanged over the planned range of output.

It follows that total profit, i.e. total revenue minus total costs, similarly will be identical for each firm at the capacity level. The only difference between the firms is in the relative size of fixed costs to variable costs. In figure 5a the firm has relatively low fixed costs, whereas in figure 5b they comprise a much larger part of total costs. As can be seen from the break-even points the first firm enjoys a much greater degree of flexibility in its output than the one in figure 5b, because its output can fall much farther below the planned capacity level before it fails to cover its total costs.

Thus relatively low fixed costs give a firm a greater margin of safety in varying its output in the short run. Relating this point to insurers, an organisation like a Lloyd's underwriting syndicate dealing exclusively through brokers and with low overheads could far more easily withstand a fall in premium income than a company with a large branch organisation geared to obtain its business direct from the public.

On the other hand relatively high variable costs will tend to produce a sharper short-run reaction to a change in the *price* at which a firm's product can be sold. As noted when discussing opportunity cost, in the short-run, so long as revenue is at least sufficient to cover variable cost, it will pay a firm to continue production because any revenue in excess of total variable cost will make some contribution towards the (unavoidable) fixed costs. Other things being equal, the higher is average variable cost (i.e. $\dfrac{\text{total variable cost}}{\text{total output}}$) relative to price, the smaller will be the possible relative fall in price before revenue is insufficient to cover variable costs, at which point it will pay a firm to cease production immediately and switch resources to new uses unless some improvement in the price can be obtained. In the long run, when there has been sufficient time to readjust all resources, any firm, whatever the pattern of its costs, will cease to produce a commodity unless its price is adequate to cover total costs; the difference is that a firm with relatively high variable costs will tend to reach that decision sooner should market price begin to fall.

Profit in relation to costs

In the last paragraph the statement that in the long run price must be sufficient to cover total costs if a firm is to remain in business implied a basic principle employed by economists. That is, the level of profit which is necessary to keep a firm in its present line of business should be treated as a cost, being included with other fixed costs. This is a corollary of the opportunity cost concept because such a level of profit (often called normal profit) is regarded as being equal to the amount of profit which could be earned, subject to the same degree of risk, by transferring the firm's resources to the best alternative use. Treating normal profit as part of fixed costs has two advantages: (1) it draws attention to the level of revenue which it is necessary for the firm to earn at any level of output in order to justify remaining in its existing business; and (2) it emphasises the fact that until all resources are earning at least what they could earn elsewhere it is not possible to talk of the firm as earning a profit. This is an important principle; for example, a small broker should impute a wage for his own services to the business before calculating his profits.

Marginal costs

Marginal cost is of particular importance in studying the behaviour of costs in relation to a change in output, it being defined as the increase in total cost resulting from the production of one more unit of a commodity[100]. Often in business usage the term incremental cost is preferred, so emphasising the concern with finite rather than infinitesimally small changes, and though it is recognised that in practice it is often impossible to estimate the effect of a change of one unit, here the term marginal cost will be used throughout for the sake of consistency.

One difficulty which arises when trying to apply the concept to insurance is that even when dealing with a particular class of insurance there is no generally accepted view as to what constitutes a unit of output for an insurance company. Though the numbers of policies issued provide a readily identifiable item [101] they are a poor, and perhaps even a misleading, measure of output, often carrying widely differing premium in recognition of substantial differences in the insurance protection afforded and the administration costs borne by the insurer. In chapter 1, insurance was defined as a device for the transfer of particular risks to an insurer. Therefore, in order to continue the analysis of an insurer's costs the unit of output used will be defined in terms of a unit of risk. In practice this may seem a rather abstract concept, embracing all of the difficulties which have been discovered in trying to identify "exposure units" for the purpose of the annual returns to the Department of Trade and Industry [102]. One solution could be to define a risk unit in terms of units of loss expectancy transferred to the insurer measured as follows:

$$\text{Loss expectancy (E)} = q \times \bar{c}$$
where
q = probability of the insured event occurring
$\bar{c}$ = the average loss if the insured event occurs.

---

[100] Using symbols, marginal costs may be defined as:
$$MC_n = TC_n - TC_{n-1}$$
where the marginal cost of producing the nth unit (MC_n) is equal to the total cost of n units (TC_n) minus the total cost of n less one units (TC_{n-1}). Alternatively it may be shown as:
$$\frac{\Delta TC}{\Delta Q}$$
where the Greek capital letter delta (Δ) means "the change in", and Q = total quantity produced.

Because fixed costs do not vary with changes in output, short-run marginal cost is a function solely of variable cost. Moreover a change in fixed costs, e.g. a rent revision for leased property, does not affect marginal cost.

[101] F. C. Knight, for example, attempted to measure labour efficiency for all classes of business by using policies in force. "Insurance Productivity" *Journal of Chartered Insurance Institute*, vol 61 (1964).

[102] In conjunction with the Claim Frequency Analysis Statement, note 5 of Schedule 3, Part 1 of the Insurance Companies (Accounts and Forms) Regulations 1968 concedes that the column "Units of Exposure" need only be completed for motor vehicle business.

This is a well known formula for the purposes of calculating premiums[103], giving the pure loss portion of the gross premium. So, for example, in life business q would be obtained from a mortality table with $\bar{c}$ as the sum insured[104]; in fire and other property insurances where risks are far more heterogeneous, with a large number of risk factors affecting both q and c, the underwriter's objective is to express loss expectancy as a rate to be applied to the sum insured, the rate differing according to the class of risk[105].

Thus using risk units (expressed as units of loss expectancy) as a measure of output, for each class of business each additional unit accepted would add the same amount to expected claims costs as all previous units. The marginal claims cost, therefore, would be constant whatever the number of risk units underwritten; in figure 5c this is shown as a line drawn parallel to the x-axis.

Table 5c

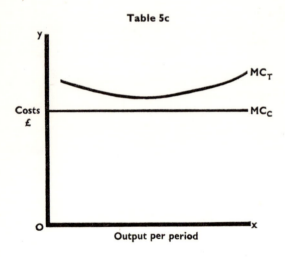

It may be assumed that variable costs associated with management expenses would be subject to diminishing returns, so that both the marginal cost and average cost curves would conform to the

---

[103] See, for example, R. E. Beard "Statistics in motor insurance" *Journal of Chartered Insurance Institute,* vol 64 (1967).
[104] In order to obtain the net premium to be charged account would also be taken of interest which would be earned on the life fund.
[105] See J. P. Weber "Realism in rating" p205 *Journal of Chartered Insurance Institute,* vol 63 (1966).

normal short run U-shapes [106]. Although an insurance company possesses a fairly wide flexibility as to the amount of business it can handle, in the short run there is a limit due to the amount of overtime which can be worked, the extra staff that can be employed in existing office accommodation, and the capacity of office equipment.

Except for the first year initial commission for some types of life business, agents' commissions are fixed as a percentage of the premium which itself is based on the risk unit as defined above. Therefore, for each additional unit of output commission will add a constant marginal cost.

Adding together all of the marginal cost items would raise total marginal cost (MC_T) above the marginal claims cost (MC_C) as shown in figure 5c.

Finally in figure 5d the average variable cost and average total cost curves are added. The high proportion of variable costs to total costs, and in turn the relatively high proportion of constant variable costs in most classes of insurance business would produce a set of cost curves all relatively close together.

Figure 5d

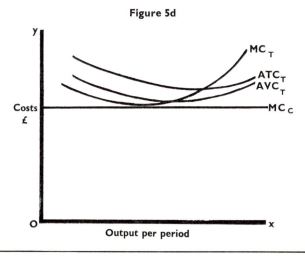

[106] The law (or more correctly, the hypothesis) of diminishing returns simply states that as more units of a variable factor are put to work with a fixed factor, after a certain point the extra production resulting from the same additions of extra inputs will become less and less. The reason is that the additional units of the variable factor have a declining share of the fixed factor with which to work. Consequently unless there is a proportionate fall in factor prices, marginal and average costs will begin to rise. An alternative explanation is provided by the law of variable proportions which demonstrates that as a firm departs from the optimal factor combination for the planned output, so marginal and average costs will rise.

Variations in long-run costs

As noted above, in the long run a firm is free to vary all of the factors of production it employs, and so can respond to what appear to be permanent changes in demand for its product by readjusting its planned capacity, selecting the least-cost method of production. Thus in the long run its costs for the planned level of output will be unaffected by diminishing returns; instead it will be able to take advantage of any economies of scale which may be available [107].

In recent years there has been considerable questioning within the industry as to the scope for economies of scale in insurance operations, and a reduction in costs has been given as one of the reasons for several major mergers. In fact the empirical evidence as to the availability of substantial economies is as slender as the theoretical arguments.

The main limiting factor is the proportion of claims to total costs, and the fact that the actual losses sustained on a portfolio of risks are largely independent of the size of the insurer. As noted in chapter 2, an insurance company may exercise some influence over losses by its loss prevention activities, but these are not necessarily a monopoly of large companies. The scale of an insurer's operations is of more importance in relation to the size of the random fluctuations in its claims experience, but even this benefit is of limited value in view of the availability of reinsurance facilities for even the smallest companies at little extra net cost.

Thus the scope for economies of scale is largely confined to sales and management expenses, though the practice of remunerating agents by means of a commission based on the premium paid further limits the proportion of total costs amenable to any economies. Variations in commission rates paid by different insurers for the same class of business are a function not directly of the size of the insurer but of its reputation and marketing policy and methods. Sometimes high commission rates are associated with lower management expenses as the result of brokers undertaking more of the work normally carried out at insurance company

---

[107] "Economies of scale" refers to the variations of cost in response to long-run changes in output using the least-cost methods of producing each level of output. If as a firm's scale of production is increased average total cost (i.e. $\frac{TC}{Q}$) falls the firm will be enjoying economies of scale with decreasing costs; conversely increasing (average) costs indicate that diseconomies of scale are operating.

Such economies/diseconomies of scale arise from the methods of production that are available to the firm as it changes its scale of output and any changes in the prices it has to pay for its factors.

For a good, short, theoretical treatment of the subject which examines the grounds for assuming that diseconomies of scale do not arise after a certain size has been reached see R. G. Lipsey, *An introduction to positive economics*, Appendix to chapter 20.

branch offices; again, however, this is independent of the size of the operation.

It must be concluded, therefore, that for most classes of insurance business no more than 20 per cent of total costs can be influenced by the scale of operation. Subject to this important qualification it is reasonable to expect that insurance operations lend themselves to a number of scale economies. To a limited degree these may be external to the individual firm, such as the development of specialist reinsurance companies, professional bodies concerned with the training of staffs, and trade associations undertaking the collection and analysis of loss data on a collective basis. The main economies, however, will be of an internal nature, the operations offering probably the greatest scope for increasing efficiency being as follows:

(1) Extensive policy, claims, accounting and other records must be maintained and analysed. The larger the company the more use it can make of mechanical and electronic equipment. This advantage, however, has been reduced by the development of computer centres from which computer time can be purchased.

(2) The sales expenses of a large company may be lower than for a small company. Goodwill is a most important asset of an insurance company, and a large company with established local connections will tend to attract business which would require more effort from a small company, though some small companies acquire a substantial reputation in specialised classes of business.

(3) The larger the company the larger the risks it can retain for its own account. The expenses of handling an individual risk do not necessarily increase in proportion to the premium; certain administration costs remain virtually the same whatever the size of the premium[108]. Also in order to secure the same stability of claims experience it will need to pass on less of its business to reinsurers.

(4) As a company grows it can achieve a greater division of labour and fully utilise specialist staff, such as surveyors, underwriting, claims and investment staffs. Again, however, it is possible for smaller companies to share specialist services.

Unfortunately it is not possible to test these hypotheses satisfactorily for the British market. Without access to internal data the best that can be achieved is to use the combined commission/expense ratios[109] from published revenue accounts which cover both UK and overseas business. As a measure of inter-company efficiency such ratios must be treated with extreme caution for a variety of reasons which have been fully discussed by Professor Lengyel[110]. Briefly, the expenses incurred by an insurer vary

---

[108]   See J. P. Weber, *op cit*, p230.

[109]   i.e. $= \dfrac{\text{commissions} + \text{management expenses}}{\text{net written premiums}}$

[110]   S. J. Lengyel *Insurance accounts: an economic interpretation and analysis* Chapter VI F. W. Cheshire Pty. Ltd. (1947).

according to the classes of business transacted; the proportion of direct to reinsurance business; the service provided; the countries of operation; the rate of expansion of the business; etc. Also the expenses shown in the published accounts will be influenced by differences in the treatment of certain items (particularly overseas taxation); their allocation between revenue and profit and loss accounts; and, in dealing with particular classes of business, the allocation of overheads between revenue accounts. Finally by expressing expenses as a ratio to premiums the resulting figure will be influenced by differences between insurers in the rates of premium charged.

Insufficient information is published to isolate the influence of each of the above factors on overall expenses to enable adequate adjustments to be made to produce perfectly comparable results. In preparing table 5.3 the base data was taken from the summaries of company results published annually by the *Policy Holder Insurance Journal* which, as far as possible, standardises the treatment of pensions and overseas taxation; also specialist reinsurance companies have been excluded. However the results still cover both home and overseas business and even between the

Table 5.3

Combined commission and expense ratios (as a percentage of world-wide written premiums) of British Insurance companies

	1962-64 (average of 3 years)			1969		
	Number of companies	Mean %	Standard Deviation %	No. of coys	Mean %	Standard Deviation %
Fire insurance						
Fire premium income:						
£0— 0·99 million	26	41·9	10·0	N.A.	N.A.	N.A.
£1— 9·99 million	11	44·0	5·4	N.A.	N.A.	N.A.
£10—49·99 million	9	45·1	2·3	N.A.	N.A.	N.A.
£50 million and over	1	44·7	—	N.A.	N.A.	N.A.
Accident insurance						
Accident premium income:						
£0— 0·99 million	18	34·7	7·6	N.A.	N.A.	N.A.
£1— 9·99 million	15	35·5	4·6	N.A.	N.A.	N.A.
£10—49·99 million	11	36·4	2·8	N.A.	N.A.	N.A.
£50 million and over	4	34·4	2·1	N.A.	N.A.	N.A.
Fire & accident insurance						
Combined fire & accident premium income:						
£0— 0·99 million	18	38·6	11·4	19	36·8	8·7
£1— 9·99 million	17	37·1	5·3	23	36·1	7·3
£10—49·99 million	9	38·5	3·5	8	34·8	5·4
£50 million and over	4	37·7	2·9	8	35·4	0·8
Motor insurance						
Motor premium income:						
£0— 0·99 million	11	36·7	11·0	18	36·8	17·1
£1— 9·99 million	14	34·8	3·4	19	34·0	5·9
£10—49·99 million	10	35·1	2·1	8	33·6	2·2
£50 million and over	2	31·2	0·7	2	30·5	1·4

Source: compiled from
Fire, Accident and Motor Underwriting Results
1962-64: *Policy Holder Insurance Journal* 4 Nov. 1966.
Fire and Accident Underwriting Results 1969—
Policy Holder Insurance Journal 27 Nov. 1970.
Motor Underwriting Results
Policy Holder Insurance Journal 4 June 1971.

leading companies there are substantial differences in the geographical distribution of their business. Moreover the combined fire and accident results make no allowance for very substantial differences between the companies in the relative importance of different classes of business transacted; as can be seen from the separate results for 1962-64, the expense ratios vary significantly between fire and other classes of business. Following the new accounting regulations introduced under the 1967 Companies Act the companies ceased to include separate fire and accident revenue accounts in their published accounts so that it is not possible to include in the table separate fire and accident figures for 1969. To a certain extent it would be possible to eliminate the effects of some of these causes of variation by the statistical process of standardising the results but this would in itself be a major research task.

Having made all of these qualifications, clearly as a measure of economies of scale available in the industry table 5.3 must be interpreted with considerable reservations. One very practical point is that all but one of the 1969 figures show a reduction on the combined average commission/expense ratios for 1962-64. One interpretation of this fact is that under the pressures of competition the industry was forced to find economies at all levels of operation at a time when salaries and many other expenses were rising, including the introduction of Selective Employment Tax in 1966. If this is the correct interpretation then it suggests that with further radical changes in methods of operation it may be possible to achieve yet more economies. A less charitable view would be that falling ratios can be attributed largely to changes in premium rates which throughout the latter part of the period were tending to rise in almost all of the major territories where British insurers operate. Without more information it is impossible to say with certainty which is the correct interpretation, but there are grounds for attributing a substantial part of the improvement to the positive steps taken by many companies to increase efficiency of operation.

At first sight the 1962-64 figures for the smallest companies in the fire insurance and accident insurance sectors of the table may appear to refute the availability of economies of scale. However, as the standard deviations reveal, in all sectors there is a much greater variation in the ratios for these small companies. This may be attributed to a number of factors:

(a) they include a number of specialist offices;
(b) some of the offices have special connections, including captive companies, which considerably reduce their sales costs; and
(c) others are Lloyd's fringe companies.

Therefore, the overall product/service mix of these small offices is not comparable with that of the larger companies. If the table had been restricted to companies whose methods of operation and product mixes had conformed more closely to the pattern of the larger companies, then it is reasonable to assume that their results would have yielded more meaningful data for the present purpose. As it is, the low costs of some of these small companies raise the question whether the larger companies by adopting some of their methods of operation could operate more efficiently.

Yet even if the smallest companies are ignored the results do not provide very convincing evidence of economies of scale being present. Indeed the 1962-64 figures for fire business, and for fire and accident insurance, show that the mean commission/expense ratios of the companies in the £1 million—£9.99 million premium income category were slightly lower than those of the largest companies, though it would be rash to infer from this that diseconomies of scale may occur at a fairly low level of output.

Using the Student's t-distribution to test the differences between the means of the expense ratios of the companies in the three largest size groups shown in table 5.3, very few of the results prove to be statistically significant[111]. The most convincing evidence of economies of scale is provided by the motor results where the difference between the mean expense ratios of the two largest groups of companies is statistically significant at the 1 per cent level for both 1962-64 and 1969; i.e. the probability that the differences could have occurred by chance is only one in a hundred. The only other support for the hypothesis that expense ratios decline with an increase in the size of company is the difference between the accident business results of the two largest groups which is significant at the 5 per cent level. Much the same results are produced by a two-way analysis of variance test. Apart from proving that expense ratios vary significantly between the different classes of business, the results do not reveal any statistical significance in the variations within each class of business. The closest the results come to revealing an acceptable level of significance is in the case of motor business.

On the other hand the hypothesis that economies of scale exist cannot be rejected by these results alone. It is noteworthy that the measure of variance employed, the standard deviation, in every case becomes smaller with the increase in the size of the companies, and using the F-distribution test, the differences in the variances prove to be statistically significant at the 5 per cent level in three cases. This may be interpreted as indicating that as the size of firm increases scale economies possibly begin to level out.

Also there is some evidence that table 5.3 does not fully reveal the full extent of the economies which are available. The sector

---

[111] Although all of the conditions were not met for a classical test to be completely suitable, it is considered that the t-test would yield more meaningful results than the available non-parametric tests.

which provides the most significant results is motor where the underlying figures come from a more nearly homogeneous class of business than the remainder, with the possible exception of fire business. Also all of the figures are calculated from the companies' world-wide results and though most of the companies obtain half or more of their non-life business from abroad, in many countries their scale of operations is relatively small which may inflate their overall commission/expense ratios. Therefore, if separate British underwriting results were available the differences between the small and the large companies may have been larger.

Support for this view is provided by an analysis of American non-life companies by R. J. Hensley. Dividing the companies into joint stock companies and mutuals, Hensley found differences of 6 points (43.9 per cent to 37.9 per cent) and 12 points (32.4 per cent to 20.4 per cent) respectively between the smallest and largest companies in each group, and a non-parametric significance test showed the differences to be significant at the 1 per cent level[112].

Similarly an analysis of New Zealand statistics (see table 5.4) reveals substantial reductions in the combined commission/expense ratios between the groups of the smallest and the largest companies despite the overall scale of operations being very small in relation to the British and American markets. These latter figures, however, must be treated with caution being based on only

Table 5.4
Expense ratios of companies operating in New Zealand during 1963/4

Nett Premiums in New Zealand	Number of companies	Mean Commissions	Mean Expenses	Mean Total	Standard Deviation
		(as percentage of premiums)			
Fire Insurance					
Fire prems.—					
under £100,000	42	7·1	46·0	53·1	31·3
£100,000/250,000	15	9·0	32·4	41·4	6·7
£250,000/500,000	2	9·3	18·6	27·9	21·7
over £500,000	3	10·4	20·1	30·5	2·5
Accident Insurance					
Accident prems.—					
under £100,000	32	9·4	29·3	38·7	17·1
£100,000/250,000	21	9·6	21·2	30·8	9·8
£250,000/500,000	14	10·2	19·1	29·3	11·2
over £500,000	10	5·9	16·2	22·1	7·6

Source: Tables 14, 15, 27 and 28 of *Insurance Statistics*, 1963/4. The New Zealand Govt. Department of Statistics.

[112] R. J. Hensley *Competition, Regulation and the Public Interest in Non-life Insurance*, p40f, University of California Press (1962).

one year's results, and not having been checked for variations in sales methods or reinsurance arrangements.

A final piece of evidence supporting the existence of economies of scale in the industry is provided by Professor J. Johnston's analysis of the 1952 ordinary life expense ratios (including commissions) of 61 British companies[113]. In view of the substantial differences in the composition of the business of individual companies, although the negative correlation coefficient between expense ratio and the logarithm of total annual premiums proved to be significant at the 5 per cent level he did not regard this as sufficient proof that costs fall with an increase in size. Therefore, he conducted further tests to eliminate the effects on costs of variations in (a) the amount of new business and (b) the volume of group life and pensions business transacted by the companies. These led him to conclude that for ordinary life business there is a significant relation between size and expenses with "the expense ratio declining on the average with increasing size of company."[114]

As labour costs form the major part of the management expenses, the possibility of increasing returns to labour are of particular importance. In a paper read to the 1963 annual conference of the Chartered Insurance Institute, F. C. Knight (an assistant manager of the Commercial Union group) attempted to measure labour efficiency for all classes of business on the basis of policies in force/employees (see Table 5.5)[115].

Table 5.5
Labour utilisation of a selected group of British insurance companies measured by policies in force

Size of companies in investigation	Ratio of policies to employees
Companies with under I million policies	327
Companies with between I & 7m policies	530
Companies (industrial and industrial-composite) with over 7 million	1,173

Source: F. C. Knight, "Insurance Productivity".

Knight himself was careful to detail the many qualifications to the table, which mainly can be summarised as follows:

(a) Different kinds of business entail different levels of service. A motor portfolio is certain to make heavy demands for policy alterations and claim investigations.

(b) The derivation of the business can cause variations. A broker-fed office could have a different policy ratio from one which procures its business by direct canvassing.

(c) The permanence of life contracts, as contrasted with the transient nature of travel insurance, affects any comparison.

---

[113] *Statistical Cost Analysis* McGraw Hill Book Co. (1960)
[114] *op cit*, p109.
[115] F. C. Knight "Insurance Productivity", *Journal of Chartered Insurance Institute* vol 61 (1964).

Since 1963 there has been a considerable rethinking in the industry; for example, with motor business now it is well recognised that much of the work involved can be handled very cheaply. Consequently today the statistics would be accepted as no more than a broad indication of the availability of increasing returns to labour. Even for fire and accident business not only must account be taken of the number of policies, and likely alterations and claims, but also the complexity of the operations involved, which determine how much of the work can be performed by a computer. Moreover, the final labour cost will be influenced too by the type of labour required, which also may provide scope for scale economies; for example, if, as a company grows, it can break down work into simple routine operations it will be able to use more mechanical and electronic equipment and so replace some of its highly trained staff with cheaper labour. Therefore, in principle Knight's conclusions that there are economies of scale to be achieved in the use of labour still appear correct.

So evidence which can be gleaned from published information indicates that small but significant economies of scale, possibly exceeding 5 per cent but certainly not more than 10 per cent of premiums, can be achieved by an optimal-scale company operating on a conventional branch office system. Possibly some savings may be achieved even beyond the size of the present largest group, but no evidence can be offered to support this proposition.

Therefore, after attaining a relatively low level of output a non-life insurer may expect the slope of its long-run average cost curve to be fairly flat, as in the figure 5e. However, average costs can be expected to fall gently up to a relatively high level of output, so that the minimum optimal scale (i.e. that level of output at which average cost is at its lowest attainable point) will represent a significant share of the total market demand for each class of insurance.

Figure 5e

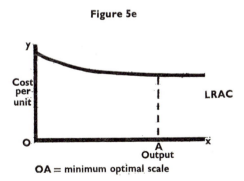

OA = minimum optimal scale

Chapter 6: The Demand for Insurance

If the analysis of costs is the first stage for a firm in arriving at rational output and pricing decisions, the second must be an understanding of the nature of the demand for its product.

Demand means more than simply a desire on the part of consumers for a particular product; for demand to be effective such desire must be coupled with an ability and a willingness by consumers to pay the price. This may seem an obvious point but it is one which producers overlook at their peril. Therefore, demand may be defined as the amount of a product which consumers are prepared to buy at a given price over a stated time period, i.e. per day, month, etc. Price obviously has a bearing on the amount of a product which consumers are willing to buy, and therefore the quantities demanded at different prices can be tabulated in a demand schedule. Theoretically by adding together the demand schedules of individual consumers it is possible to obtain a market demand schedule and the result can be expressed as a market demand curve, as in figure 6a. In practice it is far from easy to estimate accurately the demand for any product at differing prices.

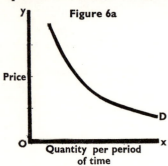

In this chapter it is proposed to consider the determinants of total market demand for insurance and the demand curve of the individual firm.

Determinants of demand for insurance

To consider first the individual consumer, his demand for any product will be influenced by many factors; the most important generally are recognised as being:

    (i) the price of the product;
    (ii) the prices of other products;
    (iii) his tastes and preferences; and
    (iv) his income.

In addition to the above, market demand is influenced by yet other factors. These include the size and age/sex composition of the population, the size of the national income and its distribution between different groups in society; and the distribution of the national wealth.

In order to simplify the task of analysis it is proposed to employ the device frequently used in economic theory of assuming that only one of the factors varies while all of the others are held constant—or as it is frequently expressed, *ceteris paribus*, i.e. all other things remaining unchanged. First the relationship between the demand for insurance and its price will be examined.

Demand and the price of insurance

Economists have sought to explain by means of the diminishing marginal utility and marginal rate of substitution theories of consumer behaviour the observed fact that the demand for a product generally varies inversely to its price[116].

The basic demand for insurance arises from the satisfaction a consumer gains from the increase in financial security achieved by transferring the risk of loss to an insurer, the opportunity cost being the satisfaction which he could have obtained from an alternative use of the premium paid. Thus when deciding whether to buy insurance the consumer is faced with the same problem as applies to the purchase of any other commodity; will the satisfaction gained be worth the price? The decision whether or not to buy insurance is complicated, however, by the fact that at the time of purchase the consumer obtains only a promise of security against loss(es) of unknown timing and extent, of which often he possesses only the vaguest probability estimates. The rational consumer, whether an individual or firm, would give priority to insuring those risks which he estimates (regardless of how subjective the estimating process may be) as having high expected loss values because either the probability of occurrence is high, or if a loss does occur it is likely to be of a catastrophic size relative to his financial resources.

Obviously the decision whether to buy insurance is influenced by personal attitudes to risk, some individuals placing far greater value on security than others. Expressed in terms of marginal utility[117], given identical information regarding loss expectancies, two individuals may choose different courses of action because one, perhaps subconsciously, applies a higher discount rate to future expected losses than the other, so calculating that he would lose less marginal utility from expected future losses than he would incur in paying the premium. When, as is often the case, the individual possesses very little statistical information regarding a risk, so being forced to rely on largely subjective estimates both of loss frequencies and of potential variations in actual results, then a reckless man may be inclined to grossly underestimate the risk whereas a cautious man may err in the opposite direction. Given such variations in personal attitudes to risk and demand for insurance, the decision whether to buy insurance will still depend

---

[116] For a discussion of these two theories see, for example, R. H. Leftwich *The price system and resource allocation*, 3rd edition, chapters 4 & 5 Holt, Rinehart & Winston (1966).
[117] i.e. the extra satisfaction provided by one more unit of a product.

finally on the rate of premium required relative to the consumer's estimate of the expected loss and of the variation in the outcome of the event to be insured. The lower the premium rate the greater the incentive to insure. Moreover a reduction in premium rates (due to insurers cutting their expenses and profit loadings) will encourage consumers to extend the range of risks which they consider it is worth while insuring. At the one end of the loss probability scale a lowering of premium rates may make it economic to insure risks with higher probabilities of loss in order to substitute the certainty of the amount and timing of a premium for the uncertainty of actual losses, even though they occur fairly regularly and individual amounts involved are relatively small. Conversely if the premium rate is closely related to the loss expectancy it may be decided to insure risks with a very remote probability of loss but of a potentially catastrophic nature, e.g. earthquake risk in the United Kingdom.

One may argue that it is the largest consumers of insurance who are the most sensitive to changes in premium rates. Large industrial and commercial firms have access to expert advice and in the case of some risks (e.g. breakdown of electric motors, and breakage of plate glass) may be able to calculate their own loss expectancies with a fair degree of accuracy. Consequently an increase either in premium rates, or in the premium discounts allowed for excesses [118], unrelated to any change in the underlying loss expectancies, may induce such firms to assume more of their own risks.

On the other hand, over a narrow band the demand for insurance may be relatively insensitive to premium changes for a number of reasons. Earlier it was stated that the basic demand for insurance lies in the demand for financial security. Firms that operate to carefully controlled capital budgets may also prefer the certain cash outflow of a premium in contrast to the uncertain timing of even relatively small losses, so being willing to accept a small increase in premium rates without reducing their demand for insurance. Similarly in some classes of insurance considerable value is placed on the ancillary services provided by the insurer; e.g. from an industrial or public relations point of view a firm stands to gain considerably from being able to hand over to an insurance company for negotiation and settlement any claims brought against it by injured employees or members of the public.

Compulsory insurance

The most important interference with the relationship of demand to the price of insurance is the existence of compulsory and quasi-compulsory insurance requirements.

The commonest example is motor insurance. Most countries

---

[118] With an excess the insured himself bears the first £x of any loss.

have enacted legislation requiring the owners and/or users of motor vehicles to insure with authorised insurers (sometimes a state monopoly) against liability to third parties. It is true that some governments also exercise control over the premiums that can be charged, but this does not alter the position that so long as insurance premiums remain a relatively small part of the total cost of motoring, total market demand for compulsory insurance cover will be independent of its price. So, for example, when passenger liability insurance becomes compulsory in Britain in December 1972[119] motorists unable to obtain cover at normal terms will no longer have the freedom of refusing to pay the higher price and still drive.

Social and political pressures on governments to guarantee protection for anyone injured through the act of another, and the development of new risks of a catastrophic nature (e.g. atomic energy and the industrial usage of nuclear materials) tend to increase the range of compulsory insurance requirements. In addition to matters dealt with by government action there are many other risks that are insured under quasi-compulsory conditions.

Insurance clauses are a common feature of many commercial contracts, e.g. mortgage and debenture deeds, leases, hire-purchase contracts, building and repair contracts, the supply of components, etc., and cover both property, liability and other types of insurances. Sometimes such contracts not only stipulate what types of insurance shall be arranged but also may specify an approved insurance company (or companies) and require that the insurance be arranged through the agency of one of the parties to the contract. For example, building societies in their mortgage deeds normally authorise the society to insure the building against fire and other perils with a company of its choice and charge the premium to the mortgagor.

Such practices are not confined solely to the private sector of the economy. In Britain compulsory insurance clauses are equally common in contracts issued by the central and local authorities and the public corporations. Although such practices destroy the freedom of choice of whether or not to insure, it may be argued that in the vast majority of cases compulsory insurance clauses on balance offer a reasonable protection for the vital interests of one or both parties to a contract, or rationalise questions of responsibility for effecting insurance against loss or injury arising out of the performance of a contract. Nonetheless, as part of the cost of securing the contract one of the parties is deprived of the right to refuse to insure if the premium is judged to be too high. This is especially important when such a clause is the common practice of the trade (e.g. building contracts containing the standard

---

[119]   Motor Vehicles (Passenger Insurance) Act 1971.

R.I.B.A. conditions), because anyone then wishing to pursue such an activity can only do so provided he complies accordingly. Of even greater significance from the standpoint of the demand for insurance is any additional restriction on the choice of insurer which prevents the person or firm from taking advantage of the premium differences which exist in a competitive market. On the other hand there is no evidence that an insurer which has been placed in the position of a monopoly supplier of insurance to a captive market (e.g. an insurance company nominated by a building society) has sought to act as a discriminating monopolist, charging higher premium rates to that group of policyholders than to the market generally.

Also, compulsory insurance requirements must be kept in perspective. Usually they stipulate certain minimum requirements, and for insurances beyond those minima market forces remain operative. So, for example, in the case of motor insurance Road Traffic Act risks comprise only a small part of the total insurance cover available to motorists.

Life insurance

In discussing the relationship of demand to the price of insurance it is also necessary to recognise the different nature of many life contracts.

Basic forms of life insurance, i.e. term and whole-life contracts, are purely contracts of insurance undertaking the payment of an agreed sum upon the death of the life insured. Thus they are concerned with meeting a demand for financial security, and between different insurers straightforward price comparisons can be made.

Today, however, most of the contracts underwritten by the life offices incorporate to a greater or lesser degree a substantial savings element in addition to insurance. Endowment policies, premium loadings for participation in profits; equity-linked and unit trust schemes are stages in the movement from insurance to what have become predominantly savings contracts as individuals seek not merely financial security for dependants but also a return for themselves on their savings. This brings a new dimension to the demand for life insurance with the life offices competing with other institutions for the savings of the personal sector of the economy, although, as noted in Chapter 3, a life office is in the fortunate position that once it has sold a new policy largely it no longer needs to compete actively for subsequent instalments of the premium because of the long-term contractual nature of life policies. However, it also means that to a large degree the demand for new life insurance contracts is at the mercy of the determinants of personal savings, notably changes in the level of income and expectations of the future.

It is essential, therefore, when discussing the demand for life insurance to recognise that the life offices deal in a range of contracts with fundamentally differing characteristics. At the one extreme is the pure insurance contract for which demand will tend to vary inversely to the price (usually expressed as a rate per cent of the sum insured). At the other extreme is the (principally) savings contract for which, *ceteris paribus*, demand will tend to vary directly with the expected rate of return on the premiums payable; in other words, again demand will tend to vary inversely to the price, now defined as a premium rate expressed as percentage of the expected maturity value.

Before leaving life insurance it should also be noted that tax concessions play a most important part in determining the net cost to the policyholder and thus its competitive position relative to other forms of savings [120]. This fact is well recognised by the life offices and brokers, it being normal practice when quoting for new insurances to show the saving of income tax the proposer will obtain assuming that the premium qualifies for the full allowance at the standard rate of tax. This has the effect of increasing demand at each level of premium.

Price elasticity

Price elasticity is concerned with the degree of responsiveness of demand for a product to a change in its price. Usually it is measured by means of the following formula which generally gives reasonably accurate results provided it is confined to relatively small changes in price:

$$\text{Elasticity of demand } (\varepsilon) = \frac{\text{percentage change in quantity demanded}}{\text{percentage change in the price}}$$

If the quotient is greater than 1 (i.e. the change in quantity is relatively larger than the change in price) demand is said to be relatively elastic; if less than 1 it is relatively inelastic; and a value of 1 means that demand is unitary elastic [121].

---

[120] The concession of allowing life premiums against income tax assessments was first given in 1799 to small incomes and subsequently extended in 1853 to all incomes.

[121] When dealing with small absolute amounts where one unit will represent a relatively large change (e.g. a change from 3 to 4 units may be interpreted as either a $33\frac{1}{3}$ per cent or 25 per cent change), it is better to employ a compromise rule using the average of the old and new quantities as the denominator so that the percentage change from 3 to 4 units becomes

$$(1 \div \frac{3 + 4}{2}) \times 100 = \frac{1}{3 \cdot 5} \times 100 = 28 \cdot 6\%$$

So, for example, if the position illustrated in figure 6b represented a price change from 3p to 4p ($=33\frac{1}{3}\%$ or 25%) and a change of quantity

continued on page 94

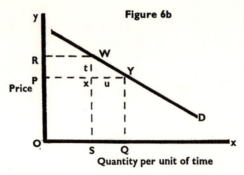

Figure 6b

y

R

P

Price

W

t

x u

Y

D

O

S Q

Quantity per unit of time

This method of measurement is illustrated in figure 6b using a linear demand curve where the increase in price from P to R reduces demand from Q to S, and the elasticity of demand is given by the formula:

$$E = \frac{\Delta q}{q} \div \frac{\Delta p}{p}$$

$$= \frac{\Delta q}{\Delta p} \cdot \frac{p}{q}$$

$$= \frac{SQ}{PR} \cdot \frac{OP}{OQ}$$

Strictly, elasticity should not be so measured over a range but at each point on the demand curve and readers familiar with differential calculus will realise that it is the derivative of quantity with respect to price; i.e.

$$E = \frac{dq}{q} \div \frac{dp}{p} = \frac{dp}{dp} \cdot \frac{p}{q}$$

Frequently elasticity is illustrated in text-books by differences

---

[1] [2] 1 continued from page 93

from 500 to 300 units ($= 40\%$ or $66\frac{2}{3}\%$), using the normal formula the result would be:

$$\frac{40\%}{33\frac{1}{3}\%} = 1\cdot2$$

However, using the same data but this time measuring for a cut in price from 4p to 3p the result becomes

$$\frac{66\frac{2}{3}\%}{25\%} = 2\cdot66$$

The compromise rule, however, would produce the same answer in either case, i.e.

$$= \frac{50\%}{28\cdot6\%} = 1\cdot75$$

in the slopes of demand curves, but except in the extreme cases of perfectly inelastic, perfectly elastic and unitary elastic demand curves (see figures 6c, d and e), this can be misleading.

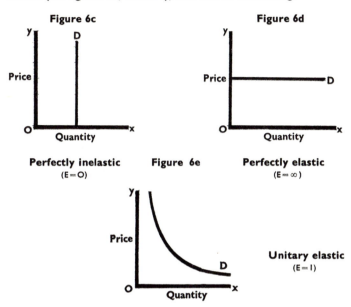

Figure 6c

Perfectly inelastic
(E = 0)

Figure 6d

Perfectly elastic
(E = ∞)

Figure 6e

Unitary elastic
(E = 1)

It is possible to prove that normally the degree of elasticity will vary over the length of a demand curve, demand generally being relatively more elastic at high prices than at low prices [122]. This is an important factor which should not be overlooked by a firm in

---

[122] In the case of a linear demand curve as illustrated in figure 6b this can be readily proved as follows. As explained above, the elasticity of demand is given by:

$$E = \frac{SQ}{PR} \cdot \frac{OP}{OQ}$$

Geometrically the slope of the demand curve at any point is given by the ratio $\frac{t}{u}$ which is equal to $\frac{PR}{SQ}$, and as the curve is a straight line this ratio will be a constant K. $\frac{PR}{SQ}$ is the reciprocal of $\frac{SQ}{PR}$ in the elasticity equation, so by substitution $E = K. \frac{OP}{OQ}$. The lower the price the larger becomes the quantity so that the value of $\frac{OP}{OQ}$ decreases. Therefore as price is reduced the numerical value of elasticity will fall over the length of the curve.

making its price/output decisions. For example, having found that a reduction in the price of its product results in a relatively large increase in the quantity demanded, a firm cannot automatically assume that a further price cut will produce the same reaction.

This concept of price elasticity is of considerable value because of the relationship between elasticity and revenue (i.e. the income produced by the sale of the product). It can be shown that the effect of a change in price on total revenue will vary according to the elasticity of demand at that point as follows:

Elasticity of demand		Change in total revenue caused by:	
		(a) a reduction in price	(b) an increase in price
Relatively inelastic	$(E<1)$	Fall	Rise
Unitary elastic	$(E=1)$	No change	No change
Relatively elastic	$(E>1)$	Rise	Fall

The explanation for this relationship is simple. If demand is relatively inelastic any change in price will result in a proportionately smaller change in the quantity sold, whereas if demand is relatively elastic then, say, a fall in price will be more than compensated for by the proportionately larger increase in quantity sold. This effect can be seen in figure 6b where a fall in the price of the product from R to P results in a loss of revenue equal to the rectangle PRWX, and a gain equal to QSXY, the difference between the two rectangles being the change in total revenue.

The relationship can be summarised in a diagram showing how total consumer expenditure (equal to total revenue for the firm(s)), varies as more of a product is demanded. As demand expands up to quantity OB in figure 6f demand is relatively elastic and total expenditure is rising. Between OB and OC demand is unitary elastic, the increase in quantity sold necessitating a proportionate reduction in price, so that total revenue remains unchanged. To the right of point OC the onset of relatively inelastic demand results in a progressive reduction in consumers' total expenditure as more units of the product are sold.

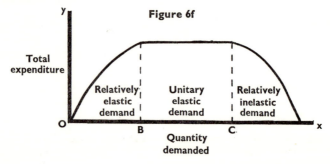

Figure 6f

The price elasticity of demand for any product is determined by a number of factors, including habit and its degree of necessity for the consumer, but by far the most important influence is the availability of substitutes. Although no other industry offers a closely competing substitute for insurance in the sense of providing a method of risk transfer, as already explained the demand for insurance is not entirely free from the influence of substitutes. In certain classes of insurance high premium rates encourage firms to devote more resources to loss prevention and exclude small losses from their insurance arrangements. Life offices have to compete with other institutions for savings contracts. On the other hand compulsory insurance requirements make demand relatively more inelastic.

So far little research has been undertaken into elasticity of demand for any class of insurance, though the breakdown of the tariff, and the need for more frequent premium revisions due to the effects of inflation on claims and management costs, have encouraged some British companies to look more closely at the problem in relation to motor insurance. It is when one considers the demand curve facing the individual insurer that the question of elasticity assumes even more importance because so far insurers in general have failed to achieve any marked degree of product differentiation. Therefore, the public tends to regard the policies of one insurer as good substitutes for similar policies offered by other insurers, so that individual insurers' demand curves probably are relatively elastic for many classes of business.

On the other hand, today more insurance companies are using competitive advertising in an attempt to establish a "brand image", and thereby persuade the public that the products offered by competitors are not close substitutes. Also it must be recognised that consumer ignorance and inertia continue to protect some companies from the full consequences of excessive premium rates (the wide range of premium rates and returns under with-profit policies offered by life offices is a case in point). Here the brokers can play a vital role. Other things being equal, it may be predicted that in principle an insurance company reliant upon brokers for its business faces a relatively more elastic demand curve than one selling direct or through part-time agents. Similarly the demand for insurance for the large commercial and industrial risks can be expected to be more price sensitive than for personal insurances because of the superior market knowledge possessed by large buyers.

Closer examination of actual behaviour would show that the influence of brokers predicted above is an over-simplification which would only hold true provided they could always be relied upon to give independent, impartial advice to clients. The common ownership links between some insurance companies and broking firms have been cited already as one threat to impartiality (pp. 19-20), but more insidious is the payment by some companies of substantially higher commission rates than those offered by competitors, without any offsetting increase in the amount of work which the broker is required to undertake for the company. On the other hand higher commission rates normally are associated with smaller and newer companies attempting to become established in the market, and using higher commissions, often in conjunction with lower premium rates, in an attempt to overcome the product differentiation advantages enjoyed by the larger established companies.

In practice it is not easy to measure elasticity of demand or to test any of the above hypotheses. It would be necessary to observe the variations in demand consequent upon changes in price, being careful to eliminate the effect of any changes in other factors influencing demand. Moreover it is essential to recognise that conditions change over time, so that conclusions based on observations at a particular moment may cease to be relevant at a later date. For example, some large companies now believe that the demand for private car insurance is less responsive to price changes than it was once thought to be, with perhaps only one tenth of the market being highly sensitive. Even if this observation is correct it calls for careful analysis. Over what price range were the observations made? Do the findings hold true of total market demand or only of the demand curves of individual insurers? Also is the lack of response a temporary phenomenon due to the uncertainty caused by a series of premium increases throughout the market as insurers seek to allow for the effect of inflation on their costs?

Despite the difficulties involved there can be no doubt about the desirability of attempting to estimate the elasticity of demand for one's product. Although an analysis of pricing is deferred to the next chapter, clearly a firm with positive marginal costs would not deliberately reduce its price if demand was known to be relatively inelastic, because by doing so its total costs would rise while total revenue would fall. The effect of a change in premium rates on the amount of business transacted, including the estimation of gains and losses, was the subject of a paper on motor insurance pricing by D. I. W. Reynolds[123]. Such estimation of gains and losses is partly an exercise in estimating price elasticity and partly a question of competitors' prices and their reactions to a price change.

The prices of other products

The relationship between the demand for a product and the prices of other products depends upon the nature of the products.

---

[123] *Motor Insurance Rate Fixing*, Institute of Actuaries Students' Society (1970).

Where they are complementary goods, such as petrol and cars, a reduction in the price of one will tend to lead to an increase in the demand for the other, as shown in figure 6g.

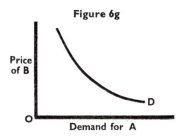

Figure 6g

Conversely in the case of two substitutes the demand for one will, *ceteris paribus,* tend to vary directly to the price of the other. This is shown in figure 6h and the more closely the two products are regarded as substitutes by consumers the flatter will be the curve.

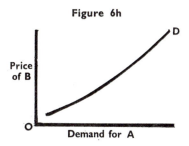

Figure 6h

The degree of responsiveness in such cases, known as the cross elasticity of demand, is given by the following formula:

$$\text{Cross elasticity of demand} = \frac{\text{percentage change in demand for commodity A}}{\text{percentage change in price of commodity B}}$$

The numerical value may be either positive (indicating substitutes) or negative (for complementary goods).

Total market demand for insurance is affected by the prices of other commodities in various ways. For example, a reduction in the cost of motoring which stimulates the demand for cars will increase the demand for motor insurance, and likewise cuts in the prices of off-peak package holidays will generate more demand for holiday insurance during the winter months. On the other hand, as already mentioned, some types of life insurance policies are exposed to substitutes through other forms of saving such as unit trusts, building society deposits, etc. In the 1960's the equity boom which substantially increased the return to existing holders of unit trusts also raised expectations regarding future performance of that type of saving, and forced the life offices to devise new equity-linked schemes of their own in order to counter the loss of business to unit trusts. To a certain degree, however, the existing business of the life offices is protected against changes in the price of substitutes by the long-term contractual nature of life policies, and the fact that surrender during the early years of a life policy will involve the policyholder in the loss of a substantial part of the premiums he has paid. Therefore any change in the relative "prices" of saving offered by other institutions will tend to change the demand for new life insurance business rather than bring about a transfer of existing business.

Cross elasticity of demand has even greater significance in relation to the demand for the policies of individual insurers who are faced with close substitutes from other insurers. The attempts of insurers to achieve product differentiation through competitive advertising already have been mentioned. Other factors bearing on the cross elasticity of demand for the various types of insurance offered by a particular insurer are:

(i) the reputation the insurer has established for efficiency of service, and especially speed and fairness in handling claims;

(ii) the inertia of policyholders and their lack of knowledge of other insurers' premium levels. Besides the influence of brokers, the periodic surveys by the Consumers' Association of different classes of personal insurance help to increase consumer awareness both of premium differentials and of differences in the scope of cover and standards of service offered by most insurers. It would be an interesting research project to study the effect on competition in the industry of the rapid growth of suburban brokers and of the work of the Consumers' Association, over the last decade.

(iii) in a market such as motor insurance where premiums are being revised with increasing frequency, the reaction of consumers to a change in competitors' premium rates will be influenced by how far they believe that the transfer of their business will result in a long-term saving of premium. It is difficult to obtain empirical evidence on such subjects, but reference may be made again to the recent experience of some of the large companies noted earlier on page 97.

(iv) most insurances are purchased at twelve-monthly or longer intervals so that there is a time-lag of up to one year before the whole body of a particular insurer's policyholders will be tempted to transfer their business as the result of a reduction in premium rates by another insurer. As noted above, the cross elasticity of demand of a life office's existing business (as opposed to new business) tends to be very low; generally the price differential must become very large before it is worth while to surrender existing policies (or convert to fully paid-up policies) and transfer to another insurer.

Changes in income levels

Changes in levels of income, whether monetary or real, have both a direct and indirect effect on the demand for insurance. Even a rise in money incomes during a period of inflation which provides no increase in the standard of living will generate additional demand for all classes of insurance as sums insured and limits of indemnity are increased to keep abreast of rising prices to maintain the same degree of security. The real growth of demand for insurance, however, comes with rising real incomes for reasons which have been tersely described as follows:

> With increasing prosperity, income above the subsistence level does not only grow absolutely, but also relatively, i.e. an ever smaller part of the income must be used in order to satisfy the physiological needs (nourishment, clothing, accommodation). That part of disposable income which exceeds the subsistence level is especially used for the purchase of durable consumer goods (furnishing, motor cars, etc.) and for services. A corresponding demand for insurance (fire, burglary, liability, etc.) develops largely parallel with these expenses. With increasing prosperity also the rate of saving increases, which in turn would be of benefit to life assurers. While the individual with a low income can spend very little or nothing at all on insurance, with rising income there is an increasing need to protect oneself against the loss of this higher standard of living: thus expenditure on insurance protection increases more than proportionately[124].

In addition economic growth brings an increase in demand from firms for insurance protection as technological advance leads to more capital-intensive methods in production and creates new risks.

The responsiveness of the demand for a product to a change in income is known as the income elasticity of demand, being measured as follows:

$$\text{Income elasticity of demand} = \frac{\text{percentage change in demand for A}}{1\% \text{ change in income}}$$

The choice of the appropriate figure for the denominator depends partly upon the nature of the product under consideration. In the case of a consumer good where demand is dependent upon personal income, the best figure to use, if the resulting information is to have any predictive value, will be "total personal disposable income *per capita*" or some variant thereof.

The numerical value of income elasticity may vary from $-\infty$ to $+\infty$ and the change in demand for a commodity caused by a change in income may take any of the forms illustrated in figure 6i.

---

[124] "An international comparison of the development of the gross national product, of private and state consumption as well as private expenditure on insurance from 1955-1968", *Sigma*, April 1971, Swiss Reinsurance Co.

102

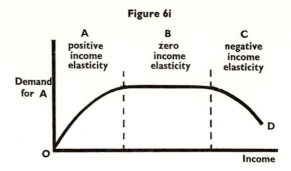

Figure 6i

Like the other elasticity measures discussed above, in practice it is difficult to obtain all of the information required to measure income elasticity of demand. Strictly, for example, the effect of variations in other determinants of demand needs to be isolated, so that the change in demand attributable solely to the change in income can be identified and used as the numerator. The longer the time period under review the more likely it is that changes in other factors besides income will have had an effect on the recorded levels of demand.

The statistics which are available do not, for the above reasons, permit precise measurement of income elasticities of demand for any particular classes of insurance. Nevertheless they do lend support to the hypothesis that rising real incomes bring about a more than proportionate increase in the demand for insurance, at least up to a certain level of income. In other words, insurers generally are operating in sector A of figure 6i.

Studies carried out by the Economics Department of Swiss Reinsurance Company have shown that in most countries where expenditure on private insurance represents a significant share of the national income, premium income per head of population has grown more rapidly than the gross national product (see table 6.1); only for three countries over the period 1965-68 was the elasticity co-efficient less than 1. In 18 of the 23 countries rising income has resulted in a more than proportionate increase in premium income per head of population. An earlier study covering the experience of 10 countries over the period 1950-66 found that in six the elasticity coefficient remained constant for the whole period; in two (Brazil and Switzerland) it was falling; in Spain it was rising for both total premiums and life premiums; and in Japan it was rising, for total premiums [125].

---

[125] "The long-term growth of insurance and the national economy", *Sigma*, October 1968. The countries covered were Brazil, France, W. Germany, Israel, Italy, Japan, Portugal, Spain, Switzerland and USA.

Table 6.1
Growth of Gross National Product and Premium Income per head
of population 1965-1968 (1965 = 100).

Col 1 Country			Col 2 1968 index of GNP per head in US $	Col 3 1968 index of premium income per head in US $	Col 4 Elasticity co-efficient (Col 3÷Col 2)
USA	..	..	122·2	123·7	1·01
Canada	..	..	122·8	118·4	0·96
Switzerland		..	120·0	126·9	1·06
Australia	..		114·4	125·7	1·10
Sweden	..		121·1	129·7	1·07
W. Germany		..	112·9	131·6	1·17
Denmark	..		118·4	127·8	1·08
Netherlands		..	128·0	127·7	1·00
New Zealand		..	88·7	101·6	1·15
Gt. Britain		..	100·4	107·0	1·07
Belgium	..	..	118·8	128·8	1·08
Norway	..	..	125·3	124·7	1·00
France	..	..	124·1	137·0	1·10
Japan	..	..	157·2	176·1	1·12
Finland	..	..	99·4	95·8	0·96
Austria	..	..	120·9	141·1	1·17
Ireland	..	..	106·7	109·7	1·03
Israel	..	..	106·3	121·0	1·14
Italy	..	..	125·4	140·7	1·12
South Africa		..	117·9	110·4	0·94
Spain	..	..	116·9	127·8	1·09
Portugal	..	..	129·7	141·7	1·09
Venezuela	..	..	108·6	129·2	1·19

Source: *Sigma*, April 1971

The Swiss Reinsurance Company's statistics also show that there is a close relationship between the level of expenditure on private insurance per head of population and the standard of living (measured by gross national product *per capita*). In table 6.2 (page 104) the countries are arranged in descending order of premium income per head: the apparently strong relationship between standards of living and insurance expenditure is confirmed by the rank correlation coefficient of 0.9562 between columns 4 and 5, which is significant at the 1 per cent level.

International comparisons such as the above need to be interpreted with great care, however, because of the range of government, social and other influences bearing on the amount of expenditure on private insurance in different countries, such as differences in compulsory insurance regulations, the range of social insurance schemes, the effect of tax allowances and changes on premiums, the marketing arrangements of insurers, etc. Consequently two countries may have similar elasticity coefficients for very different reasons. Likewise past experience may prove to be a very poor guide to the future if conditions change in the meantime.

To turn to the UK market, only since 1969 has data become

Table 6.2
The most important insurance countries of the world, 1969.
(Domestic life and non-life premiums)

Col 1	Col 2	Col 3	Col 4	Col 5
	Premium		Average values per head of population	
Country	income US $ billion	As % of GNP	(US $) Premiums	(US $) GNP
USA..	61·7	8·0	303·8	3,814
Canada	3·3	5·9	156·7	2,646
Switzerland	0·9	5·9	145·7	2,490
Australia[1]	1·6	6·5	126·7	1,944
Sweden	0·9	3·9	117·3	2,983
West Germany	6·7	5·3	111·1	2,115
Denmark ..	0·5	4·5	98·3	2,118
Netherlands	1·2	5·4	96·5	1,795
New Zealand	0·3	6·3	93·6	1,484
Gt. Britain[2]	4·7	5·6	84·6	1,518
Belgium	0·8	4·5	82·5	1,835
Norway	0·3	4·1	80·0	1,932
France	4·0	4·0	79·0	1,963
Japan[3]	6·4	4·8	62·5	1,296
Finland	0·3	3·7	55·7	1,525
Austria	0·4	4·2	53·2	1,263
Ireland	0·1	5·1	46·9	914
Israel	0·1	3·4	43·6	1,301
Italy	1·6	2·4	30·3	1,245
South Africa	0·6	4·5	30·2	673
Spain	0·6	2·6	19·5	741
Argentina ..	0·4	2·0	16·8	830
Portugal	0·1	2·7	13·4	504
Venezuela ..	0·1	1·6	13·3	841
Mexico	0·3	1·0	5·4	556
Philippines	0·1	1·7	3·1	180
Brazil	0·3	1·2	3·0	257
Pakistan	0·5	0·8	1·0	118
India	0·5	1·2	0·9	76

[1] premiums estimated
[2] 1 July 1968-69
[3] 1 April 1969-70   Source: *Sigma*, March 1971

available of UK non-life premium income [126], but for the purpose of calculating income elasticities of demand its value has been severely diminished by the regular substantial increases in premium rates which have taken place in all of the main classes of non-life insurance in recent years. Life insurance statistics are not only available for far more years but also are a more reliable guide.

It is true that the rise in market interest rates over the last two decades has reduced the price of life insurance (as defined on page 93) but at the same time increased competition from other

---

[126] This is the result of the Companies Act 1967 and the Forms Regulations which require the separation of UK and overseas premium income in the annual returns to the Department of Trade and Industry.

institutions, especially unit trusts, has exerted a counter-effect on the expansion of demand.

An examination of the premium income figures over the last 20 years shows that ordinary life business has grown far faster than industrial life insurance (see table 1.2). No doubt this can be attributed at least in part to the general rise in both money and real incomes which has enabled many of the lower paid to switch their demand from the smaller, relatively more expensive, industrial life policies to ordinary life insurance. In the language of economics, compared with ordinary life insurance, industrial life insurers are supplying an inferior good. Therefore, in table 6.3 (page 106) the premium income has been subdivided between the two classes of business. Also separate figures are provided for new business which more accurately reflects the state of current demand than total premium income; the renewal premiums of existing business form a substantial part of total premium income, and changes from year to year are affected not only by the volume of new business but also by the maturity and surrender of existing contracts. Annuity business has been excluded from table 6.3 on two grounds:

(a) the fundamentally different nature of the business: life policies basically provide security against the risk of dying young whereas annuities provide security against the risk of living too long.

(b) a substantial part of the business consists of group pension schemes, the demand for which during the period covered by table 6.3 was adversely affected by the uncertainty regarding the government's pension plans.

Averaged over the 5-year period covered by the table the elasticity co-efficients, calculated as in table 6.1, are as follows:

	Industrial life	Ordinary life	Combined
Total premium income ..	0·81	2·12	1·80
New business	1·14	3·63	3·08
New business (excluding single premiums	—	1·53	1·44

The very large increases in ordinary life new business in 1967 and 1968 were attributable mainly to a sudden surge in single premium insurances. This was curbed by the Finance Act 1968 which excluded from income tax relief policies with premiums payable for less than 10 years. It may be argued, therefore, that the figures excluding single premiums are a better indicator of the future long-term growth of demand for life insurance than the total new business premiums. It is interesting to note that the Swiss Reinsurance Company's study of the long-term growth of life insurance for the period 1950-65 produced elasticity coeffi-

Table 6.3

Growth of personal disposable income and life insurance premiums per head of population in the United Kingdom

Year	Personal disposable income per head £	Life premium income per head					
		New business			Total premium income		
		Industrial £	Ordinary £	Total £	Industrial £	Ordinary £	Total £
1964	433·02	0·51	1·86	2·37	3·60	11·35	14·95
1965	460·06	0·54	1·94	2·48	3·75	12·29	16·04
1966	484·61	0·57	2·08	2·65	3·92	13·35	17·27
1967	501·26	0·60	2·79	3·39	4·07	15·03	19·10
1968	530·10	0·64	3·37	4·01	4·25	16·73	20·98
Percentage increase over previous year	%	%	%	%	%	%	%
1965	6·24	5·88	4·30	4·64	4·16	8·28	7·29
			(3·05)	(3·85)			
1966	5·33	5·56	7·22	6·85	4·53	8·62	7·67
			(6·29)	(6·02)			
1967	3·43	5·26	34·13	27·92	3·83	12·58	10·60
			(6·33)	(6·11)			
1968	5·75	6·67	20·78	18·29	4·42	11·31	9·84
			(15·24)	(13·17)			
Percentage increase 1964-68	22·42	25·49	81·18	69·20	18·06	47·40	40·33
			(34·22)	(32·22)			

Source: compiled from National Income & Expenditure, and Insurance tables of *Annual Abstract of Statistics*, 1970.

Notes:
1. The premium income figures cover the UK business of British & foreign registered companies but omit the relatively very small business of Lloyd's syndicates.
2. The new business figures in brackets exclude single premiums.

cients of 1.474 and 1.508 for France and West Germany respectively[127].

The table clearly illustrates the difference between the growth potentials of industrial and ordinary life business. Statistics published by the Industrial Life Offices' Association show that over the period the number of new industrial life policies issued each year actually were falling and the new business coefficient of 1·14 is explained by an offsetting increase in the average sum insured.

Excluding only total industrial life premium income, although the elasticity coefficients for individual years vary, the overall trend is upwards. How long this can be sustained is questionable; in the United States demand is now growing only in line with national income, and as standards of living rise in the United Kingdom the stage may be reached where income elasticity of demand for life insurance may begin to fall. In the meantime it may be safely predicted that demand will continue to grow at a faster rate than the economy generally.

Although it is not possible to undertake the same analysis of income elasticity for non-life insurance in Britain, there is no reason to believe that its value is less than 1.

The demand curve for the individual firm

Having examined the main determinants of demand in the light of available evidence, attention can now be concentrated on the position of the individual insurer. Whatever the objectives of the firm, optimal output/pricing decisions can only be made in the light of information regarding the demand curve(s) for the firm's product(s). Professor Hague has written that "marketing is concerned with every aspect of the business"[128], and certainly, as explained in Chapter 5, the chosen scale of output will directly affect cost levels, but conversely an ability to produce a given output at a certain cost does not by itself carry any guarantee that it can be sold at any particular price chosen by the firm, and it is even less likely that the firm will thereby maximise profits.

The first step in understanding the nature of demand for the firm's own product will be to obtain as much information as possible about total market demand. Is the market static, expanding or declining? What price changes have been made and with what effect? Are there close substitutes for the product; if so, how have their producers behaved; and what influence have they had on the demand for one's own product? It is with such ques-

[127] op cit, Sigma, October 1968.
[128] D. C. Hague Managerial Economics p294 Longmans Green & Co. (1969).

108

tions that we have been concerned in the earlier parts of this
chapter, and one could go on to consider other factors such as outside influences like government regulation and legislation affecting
demand. Moreover a firm operating on an international scale
would need to look at each country individually because of likely
differences in conditions.

Armed with such information the danger to be avoided is to
treat the demand for the firm's own product as being identical
to market demand. The analysis of cross-elasticity of demand
drew attention to the influence of the prices of competitors'
products, and any firm in attempting to understand more about
the demand for its own product must pay regard to the structure
of the industry in which it operates and the market behaviour of
competitors.

In a highly competitive market composed of a large number of
small firms the individual firm will be close to the position of the
classical perfectly competitive firm, having to accept the going
market price; in other words its demand curve will be perfectly
elastic (see figure 6j). At the other extreme is the monopolist, or
the firm in such a dominant market position that it can afford to
act very much like a monopolist; its demand curve will be that of
the industry, downward sloping from left to right, and the firm will
be free to select the price which will maximise its chosen objectives (see figure 6k).

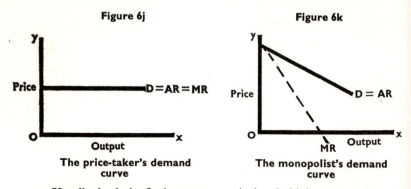

Figure 6j

The price-taker's demand
curve

Figure 6k

The monopolist's demand
curve

Usually the desire for long-term survival ranks high amongst the
chosen objectives of most firms, so that expected future levels of
demand also are important. This means that the firm must pay
regard not only to the present state of competition in the industry
but also potential competition from prospective new entrants to the
market. Therefore an evaluation of the conditions of entry to the
market will need to be undertaken by the firm.

Average and marginal revenue
Before considering the actual position of individual insurers

relative to figures 6j and 6k the demand curve counterparts of average and marginal costs can be examined.

The D curve in figures 6j and 6k has been described as the demand curve for the firm's product. Alternatively it may be called the average revenue curve. In chapter 5 average total cost was defined as $\dfrac{\text{Total cost}}{\text{Output}}$; likewise average revenue is equal to $\dfrac{\text{Total revenue}}{\text{Quantity sold}}$, which is the same as the price for each level of output.

In the same way as marginal cost measures the change in total cost resulting from a change of output, marginal revenue is equal to the change in total revenue resulting from the sale of one more unit of the product. In the next chapter the significance of marginal revenue and marginal cost will be discussed in relation to output/pricing decisions; for the moment it will be sufficient to note the relationship of marginal revenue to average revenue. In figure 6j, where the firm can sell as much or as little as it likes at the going market price, marginal revenue is equal to average revenue because each unit sold adds the same amount to total revenue. If in order to sell more the firm must lower its price, as in figure 6k, then at each level of output marginal revenue will be less than average revenue by an amount equal to the reduction in price multiplied by the number of units previously sold[129].

---

[129]   This proposition may be easily proved as follows:

(1) If N units are sold at a price of P_n, then total revenue (TR_n) will be equal to NP_n and an increase in sales by 1 unit will produce a total revenue of $(N+1)P+n1$, where P_n+1 is the price at which that output can be sold.

(2) Similarly average revenue will be equal to
$$AR_n \; = \; \frac{NP_n}{N} \; = \; P_n$$

and $\qquad AR_{n+1} \; = \; \dfrac{(N+1)\ P_{n+1}}{N+1} \; = \; P_{n+1}$

(3) The marginal revenue of the nth+1 unit will be—
$$
\begin{aligned}
MR_{n+1} \; &= \; (N+1)\ p_{n+1} \; - \; NP_n \\
&= \; NP_{n+1} \; + \; P_{n+1} \; -NP_n \\
&= \; N(P_{n+1}-P_n) \; + \; P_{n+1}
\end{aligned}
$$

That is, marginal revenue will be equal to the sum of the price of the last unit plus the product of the total number of units previously sold multiplied by the change in price.

If more units can be sold without any change in the price, i.e.
$$P_{n+1} \; = \; P_n,$$
then
$$MR_{n+1} \; = \; P_{n+1} \; = \; AR_{n+1}.$$

continued on page 110

Individual demand curves in the insurance industry

To deal specifically now with the position of the individual insurer, the first point to note is that most insurers operate in more than one market, and so are concerned with a number of different demand curves. Mention has already been made of the variations in conditions applying in different countries but in addition it is desirable for purposes of demand analysis to treat the main classes of insurance as being sold in different, even if closely related, markets. Indeed it may also be advantageous to distinguish between different types of purchaser. As noted in earlier chapters, buyers of insurance differ considerably in their knowledge of the market and their bargaining powers, and an insurer operating mainly through brokers may find that for the same class of business its demand curve is different from that of an insurer selling direct or through part-time agents.

Obviously it is impossible in the scope of this book to examine in detail more than one or two of the insurance markets. However the following discussion will illustrate the basic principles.

The one market still subject to formal price agreements is that for industrial and commercial fire insurance, which at the time of writing is under examination by the Monopolies Commission. As noted in table 1.5, the tariff companies, which include seven of the ten largest non-life groups, dominate the market, a situation which the tariff companies seek to retain by means of the so-called 65/35 per cent rule [130]. In one sense they act as price leaders, tariff premium rates being the standard against which the rates of non-tariff insurers are judged, and in an era of underwriting losses it is left to the tariff companies to restore premium rates to an adequate level [131]. Under such conditions the demand curve

---

[129] *continued from page* 109

If, on the other hand, the firms has a sloping demand curve as in figure 6k, then

$$P_{n+1} < P_n, \text{ so making } N(P_{n+1} - P_n) < 0$$

Therefore $MR_{n+1} < AR_{n+1}$

Taking a simple numerical example, assume that an increase in sales from 30 to 31 units reduces price from £4 to £3.

Therefore:

$$TR_n = 30 \times £4 = £120, \text{ and } AR_n = \frac{30 \times 4}{30} = £4$$

$$TR_{n+1} = 31 \times £3 = £93, \text{ and } AR_{n+1} = \frac{31 \times 3}{31} = £3$$

$$\text{and } MR_{n+1} = TR_{n+1} - TR_n = £27$$

$$\text{or } MR_{n+1} = 30 \times (3-4) + 3$$
$$= -30 + 3 = -£27$$

[130] This is an informal agreement between the companies not to participate in the insurance of any large fire risk unless tariff companies underwrite at least 65 per cent of total sum insured.

[131] See R. L. Carter *Competition in the British fire & accident insurance market* Ch.2.

for the individual insurer will depend on (a) whether it is a tariff or independent insurer and (b) its size.

A tariff company is required to charge not less than the prescribed rates though it may charge more. Its ability to charge more than the tariff rate will depend on the degree of product differentiation it has been able to achieve, but as the Fire Offices' Committee also regulates policy covers and wordings a reputation for product superiority must rest entirely on the quality of service provided. Therefore, in the absence of evidence to the contrary, it is reasonable to assume that demand above the minimum tariff rates will be highly elastic. At the tariff rate level the demand curve for the individual tariff company will depend upon two factors. First it will be related to the total volume of business available for tariff companies at that price, which in turn will depend upon (a) total market demand at each rate level; (b) the premium rates quoted by non-tariff insurers; and (c) the limit to non-tariff underwriting capacity and so ability to exert effective competition. Secondly, the individual tariff company will be in competition with other members of the F.O.C. for the available business; how much business it will be able to attract will depend upon its reputation relative to other tariff companies, but so long as it abides by the association's regulations it must act as a price-taker.

At this stage of the analysis it is necessary to deal with the problem that in practice premium rates vary according to the type of risk involved; the fire tariff employs a system of schedule rating with different basic premium rates (expressed as a percentage of the sum insured) applying to different classes of trades and with schedule adjustments for building construction, hazardous trade processes, fire extinguishing appliances, and other physical features affecting the overall risk. Therefore it is proposed to define price in the same manner as the concept of cost developed in Chapter 5, i.e. price will be defined as the premium rate for a standard unit of loss expectancy. Thus the above hypotheses regarding a tariff company's demand curve can be translated into figure 61.

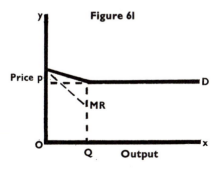

Figure 61

For a small-sized tariff company figure 6l would provide an adequate explanation of its effective short-run demand curve, because given its existing financial resources the company could exhaust its underwriting capacity at the tariff rate (assuming that the rate has been fixed at a level sufficiently low to provide tariff companies with a substantial volume of business relative to their aggregate underwriting capacity).

The larger is a tariff company's underwriting capacity the more important it is to consider its market share. So long as it remains relatively small the company can treat its demand curve as being perfectly elastic at the given tariff rate, but if in the long-run a company, perhaps through a series of mergers, secures a dominant share of the tariff market then it must consider whether further expansion could be achieved at the tariff rate or whether it would be approaching the point on the total market demand curve where demand could be expanded only by lowering its price. This raises questions regarding the survival of a price agreement in a situation of excess capacity amongst companies subscribing to the agreement, and further consideration of this must be deferred to the next chapter[132].

The position of a non-tariff insurer is somewhat different. Commercial and industrial buyers of insurance generally have access to expert knowledge of the market and of the reputations of individual insurers, so that there is little scope for a non-tariff insurer to charge above the tariff premium rate. The only hope of doing so would be by bettering the long-standing reputation of tariff companies for service and fair treatment in the handling of claims, and this seems so difficult to achieve that in the case of many non-tariff insurers their demand curve probably lies

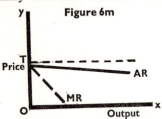

Figure 6m

entirely below the price level established by the tariff, as in figure 6m where OT is the tariff price. Exactly how far the independent insurer's demand curve will lie below OT will depend on (a) its own reputation and (b) the price of other independent insurers. For a small company the demand curve probably would be highly elastic up to its existing capacity level; two possible reasons for this assumption are that the company would be forced largely into the position of a price-taker and with a very small market share even a substantial increase in its business would not incite retaliation by competitors.

Once again it may be assumed that a very large company would be in a different situation, as illustrated in figure 6n. Its reputation may match that of the best tariff companies so that it could secure

[132] See pages 116 *et seq.*

some business above the tariff price but demand there would be highly elastic. Conversely any attempt substantially to expand its market share by cutting prices would force competitors,

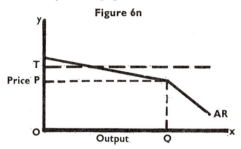

Figure 6n

including the tariff companies, to retaliate. Thus using the analysis of kinked demand curves[133], if the company was producing quantity OQ at price OP any reduction in price would not produce any substantial increase in demand whereas any increase in price would lead to a more than proportionate loss of business.

The possible reactions of competitors to any change in the price/output decisions of a firm become a matter of considerable importance for large companies controlling a substantial share of the market, and will be more fully discussed in the next chapter.

Taking life insurance as the second example, clearly life insurers operate in more than one market; group pension business is a distinctly different product from either ordinary or industrial life business. Although the latter two classes of business compete with each other at the margin, again the conditions under which they are sold are so different that it is more sensible to analyse demand for each class separately. As seen earlier the market demand for industrial life insurance is growing much more slowly than ordinary life, though the industrial life offices have not had to face the same substantial competition from new entrants or probably, the unit trusts as ordinary life.

Concentrating on ordinary life business, this is a market free of price agreements with demand growing steadily each year, but with considerable competition from outside substitutes for certain types of business. The *prima facie* homogeneity of the product (or at least each basic type of policy) would suggest that the cross-elasticity of demand between the products of different insurers is very high and that individual demand curves are highly elastic. This proposition, however, needs to be modified in the light of consumer ignorance, the differing reputations of insurers, their marketing policies, standards of selection, and, in connection with

---

[133] See P. M. Sweezy "Demand under conditions of oligopoly" in *Readings in price theory* American Economic Association, R. D. Irwin Inc. (1952).

with-profits insurances, the risk functions of consumers. Also in special circumstances it may be possible to maintain price well above the market level without substantial loss of business; for example, when the office transacts a considerable volume of mortgage business conditional upon prospective mortgagors effecting an endowment policy for a sum insured not less than the mortgage advance. Variations in policy cover offer little scope for non-price competition except in regard to the flexibility of the contract in allowing the policyholder a variety of options should his financial, etc. condition subsequently change. Finally the relative size and nature of selling costs are of importance: on the one hand advertising expenditure will seek to stimulate demand by increasing consumer awareness of an office and in the long run improve its reputation, while high commission rates will attract the attention of brokers.

Clearly though similarities may exist, the individual demand curves of offices differ and it is reasonable to assume that none is perfectly elastic. Once again the size of the office is important because it may be assumed that the larger the office's market share the less freedom of independent action it possesses in that price reductions designed to expand its share will tend to induce retaliation from competitors. Thus for the large life office the demand curve may be similar to that in figure 6n, though in the absence of any recognised tariff rate demand may be relatively less elastic to the left of quantity OQ.

At this point a distinction needs to be made between non-profit and with-profit business. With the former, apart from the question of options and surrender values, straight price comparisons can be made so that each office's demand curve is probably more elastic than for with-profit insurances where in making comparisons it is necessary to make certain assumptions, particularly regarding future bonus rates. The surveys of returns under with-profit policies made by the Consumers' Association and the *Economist* have revealed variations of up to 50 per cent between the worst and the best, so suggesting that it is possible to secure business at well above the average market price. This could be interpreted as partly a reflection of consumer attitude to risk if it could be shown that poor returns carry a substantially higher degree of certainty than high returns: no research, however, has been carried out on this subject. Therefore a small office content to write a volume of business around its existing capacity level may face a relatively inelastic demand curve for with-profits business, though a growth of consumer knowledge could imperil its position. On the other hand a small office anxious to expand would need to lower price though so long as its market share remained small in an expanding market situation its demand curve probably would be relatively elastic.

At this stage the reader may protest that all of this analysis is purely hypothetical and is unsupported by empirical evidence. Largely this is true, though some work has been done in the area; for example a study of motor insurance before the collapse of the tariff found that most non-tariff insurers, and certainly all of the larger ones, fixed basic premium rates between 5 and 10 per cent below tariff levels[134]. This evidence is based, however, on quoted prices which are not entirely the same as evidence of individual demand curves; for each company the quoted premium rate represented a point on its demand curve. This is knowledge every firm possesses; what it does not know is the position of the other parts of the curve which is important information for deciding an optimal price. How it can deal with this problem will be discussed in the following chapter.

---

[134]   R. L. Carter, *op cit*, Chapter 2.

Chapter 7: Pricing Policy and Efficiency of Operations

In this final chapter it is proposed to examine two aspects of the operations of insurance companies which involve the interests of management, shareholders and the public at large. Like other firms, an insurance company has at its disposal certain limited resources which it has to decide how to use, and the pricing policy it adopts is, of course, one of the factors which determine operations.

THE PRICING OF INSURANCE SERVICES

In choosing to discuss pricing it must not be assumed that this necessarily is the most important of the decisions an insurance management must take; indeed it is even only one part of overall market strategy, which also should include such matters as advertising, sales organisation, the usage and remuneration of intermediaries, etc. Equally important too is investment policy (especially for life operations) and claims handling. The reason for selecting pricing from amongst these other areas of decision-making is two-fold: it is of particular interest to economists, bringing together the matters discussed in the last two chapters, and it is an aspect of insurance operations which has received less attention than others by writers on insurance.

Before proceeding to analyse the elements of pricing policy, or indeed any other major area of decision-making, it is essential to consider first the context, that is the objectives of the firm.

Business objectives

Insurers come in different types and sizes, and so it may be assumed that they do not all share exactly the same objectives, or at least place them in the same order or priority. Undoubtedly it is necessary to distinguish between proprietary and mutual companies; in theory the former are operated in the interest of their shareholders whereas the latter belong to and exist to serve their policyholders. If, quite reasonably, it is assumed that shareholders are interested in the growth of dividends, then it is plausible that profit maximisation is the main motive of a proprietary company. Lacking shareholders, mutual companies obviously cannot share this objective, something else must be put in its place and this will affect their behaviour and the decisions they take[135].

---

[135] One writer has argued, however, that the main objective of a mutual life office is to make the maximum possible profit for its (with-profit) policyholders. See J. M. McDonnell, *Manpower with special reference to branch organisation*, Chartered Insurance Institute 1971 Annual Conference Paper, p.2.

In reality it is not easy to discover what are the true objectives of any company. This is not very surprising if one tries to examine one's own motives in making any particular decision, and it is further realised that over time motives may change, partially in response to changed circumstances. Translating this question of motivation into the context of a large company organisation, a further important problem arises. Rarely, if ever, does the decision making process lie in the hands of one person or even one body. Power and responsibility are divided throughout the organisational structure, so that the actions of the company may be the result of a variety of objectives, and even major policy decisions may be put into action by a body which exercises effective *de facto* rather than *de jure* control of the company. One of the important features of large companies is the extent of the separation of ownership and management, which may result in the interests of the latter supplanting those of the owners so that profit maximisation no longer represents the main motive of the company. Consequently in the insurance industry the motives of large mutual and proprietary companies need no longer differ.

Although profit maximisation is the basic hypothesis of orthodox economic analysis, in recent years this has been subject to considerable questioning on two grounds. First, various writers have cogently argued that firms may have other motives; in particular management may seek to maximise other objectives which better seem to serve their particular interests. For example they may seek to maximise either sales or the firms' market share or perhaps to maximise the rate of growth of some other aspect of the firm, such as its assets.

Secondly, it has been suggested that some firms may not be interested in maximising anything. In particular H. Simon has suggested that firms operating in an environment of uncertainty and given the difficulties and costs of obtaining all of the relevant data required to reach maximising decisions, set themselves more easily attainable targets. Such a form of behaviour has been given the title satisficing [136]. Also it must be recognised that firms may embrace other objectives, such as long-run survival, and in the insurance industry considerable emphasis traditionally has been placed on serving the public interest, though more will be said about that later.

Before examining the implications for optimal output/pricing decisions of choosing any one of these different objectives, two important points need to be emphasised.

Maximisation means more than choosing a course of action which simply improves on existing performance. It requires a management to consider all alternative courses of action and to

---

[136]   H. A. Simon "Theories of decision-making in economics" American *Economic Review* June 1959.

select the one which yields the best results. Obviously this calls for far more information than most companies have at their disposal and this fact lends support to Simon's satisficing theory, though modern mathematical techniques enable more data to be handled and rational choices made accordingly than in the past.

The second point is that a firm must make its choice from the various alternatives available. In the short run it is not possible, for example, to maximise both profits and sales, and even in the long run the firm which chooses to maximise its sales usually will earn less profit than the profit maximising company. It is true that a company may compromise between two alternative objectives, but then it ceases to maximise either.

Profit maximising

Taking the analysis of costs and revenue developed in the previous two chapters, it is now possible to ascertain the profit maximising position for a firm. It will be recalled that in the short run costs can be divided into fixed and variable costs, and that marginal cost measures the change in total cost (attributable entirely to changing variable costs) resulting from a change in output. Likewise marginal revenue measures the change in total revenue caused by a change in quantity sold. Figure 7a brings marginal cost and marginal revenue together, with MR=MC at output OQ. At any lower output MC < MR so that an increase in output adds more to total revenue than to total cost. Beyond output OQ then MC > MR so resulting in a loss on each unit sold.

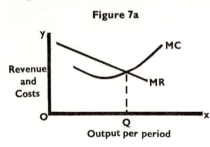

Figure 7a

Expressing this another way, by increasing output up to the level OQ the firm will maximise the contribution which the product makes towards the fixed costs of remaining in business; thus output OQ is its profit maximising output. In figure 7a the MR curve has been drawn sloping down to the right, so implying that in order to increase sales the firm must be prepared to reduce price. The reader can prove for himself, however, that a firm which is a price-taker likewise will maximise its short-run profits where MC=MR, so long as the MC curve is rising at that point. This profit-maximising relationship in fact holds true for all firms.

It must be emphasised that profit maximisation does not always mean that a firm will be earning profits. At the profit maximising point demand may be too low, or costs too high, for price to

cover both the variable and fixed costs. In such a situation, so
long as the price (i.e. average revenue) is sufficient to cover the
average variable costs, by following the profit maximising rule the
firm will be earning the maximum contribution towards its
fixed costs and so be minimising its losses. If price fell below
average variable costs, however, it would pay the firm to cease
production immediately.

Although figure 7a shows the profit-maximising output it does
not indicate either the price which should be charged or the size
of the expected profit; to obtain this information details of
average revenue and average cost are needed. Accordingly in
figure 7b at the profit-maximising output OQ the price shown by
the average revenue curve is OP, with average costs (including
normal profit) equal to OT. This gives a profit on each unit sold
of OP — OT, making a total supra-normal profit equal to the
rectangle PRST.

Figure 7b

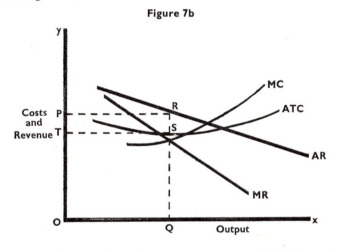

A complication frequently encountered in real life is that the
firm may produce several products, like a composite insurance
company which transacts various classes of insurance often in a
number of different countries. Given the constraints imposed by
existing resources, the object of the firm then will be to sell such
quantities of each product at such prices as will maximise its overall profits. In the short run the marginal analysis outlined above
provides a guide to how this can be achieved. If the firm attempted
to compare the net profit (i.e. total revenue—total cost) produced
by each product it would need to allocate carefully all costs
between them. This should be a relatively straight forward task with
the variable costs, but fixed costs are certain to present a number of
almost intractable problems. There just is no absolutely correct

method of dealing with many items like general management and administration costs, or some sales costs. Certain principles can be established for the sake of consistency but in the final analysis all involve certain arbitrary decisions; e.g. should fixed costs be allocated on the basis of turnover, or the relative sizes of variable costs, or labour times, or by some other method?

Using figure 7a it was shown that in arriving at short-run profit-maximising decisions what matters is the relationship of variable costs to revenue, or more precisely marginal cost to marginal revenue; fixed costs, which are unaffected by changes in the level of output, have no bearing on that decision. Therefore, in attempting to ascertain the profit-maximising price for a particular product it is simpler not to try to allocate fixed costs. Instead it is sufficient to concentrate attention on the variable costs and find what contribution the product can make towards the fixed costs. This has been called contribution pricing and is illustrated in figure 7c. The rectangle PUVW (i.e. the difference between the price and the average variable cost of quantity OQ, multiplied by the number of units sold=OQ (OP—OW), is the contribution the product would make to fixed costs. Overall profit-maximisa-

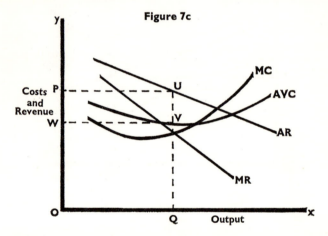

Figure 7c

tion for a multi-product firm is then achieved by equating the contributions provided by each product. If one provides a higher contribution than another, then it will pay the firm to transfer resources so as to expand the output of the more profitable product at the expense of the other.

In attempting to apply this type of marginal analysis to the operations of insurance companies there is one major complication which was ignored in the last two chapters; premium income generates a second source of income in the form of investment earnings on policyholders' funds, their relative importance varying between different classes of insurance. In life insurance the investment of the funds provides a major source of earnings for which the life offices make due allowance when calculating premium rates by discounting future expected claims payments at a rate of interest which they conservatively estimate they will be able to earn over the period (at the same time they also allow for the fact that premium payments will be spread over a number of years too).

In the case of non-life business the relative importance of investment earnings varies directly with the length of the period of insurance (usually 12 months) and the average delay in claims settlements. Although the accumulation of funds representing liabilities to policyholders is as much an integral part of non-life insurance as of life business, insurance companies generally have explicitly excluded it from their premium calculations, and have resisted attempts by state supervisory bodies (e.g. in the United States) to bring it into account, partly from fear that it may be used as a means of further depressing premium rates[137]. On the other hand, as the size of an insurer's investment earnings is directly related to the volume of business transacted and the level of premium rates charged, it cannot be ignored in arriving at optimal pricing decisions; in 1970, for example, the investment income earned by the ten leading British composite companies on their non-life funds amounted to £120·5 millions (compared with an underwriting loss of £19·2 millions), and though this did not include capital gains it was equivalent to 7·1 per cent of total net non-life premiums. Therefore, in order to adapt the above marginal analysis to allow for investment earnings on non-life business the system used by the life offices could be employed, i.e. costs could be discounted using an appropriate rate of interest. So, for example, if in dealing with annual policies it was found that claims were evenly distributed throughout the year and on average claims settlements (by amount) were subject to one year's delay, the claims costs and associated expenses would be discounted at the rate of $[1+i)^{-1\cdot5}]$, where i is the rate of interest the insurer would expect to earn on the funds. If the premium was fixed at a level sufficiently high to yield a profit on the business then additional allowance would need to be made for interest earned on the surplus until its allocation to shareholders; conversely inadequate premiums would result in a loss of investment earnings.

Ignoring the complication of the premium rate level (which in practice would have only a minor effect on total investment

---

[137] See, for example, L. H. Longley-Cook "Rate making—manual rates" pp. 40-41, in *Multiple line insurers. Their nature and operation,* ed. by G. F. Michelbacher and N. R. Roos, 2nd edition, McGraw Hill (1970).

earnings); and given the assumptions that:

(1)   the rate of investment earnings do not vary according to the size of the fund; and

(2)   expected claims costs are constant per unit of output; then the result of the suggested discounting of (expected) claims costs and associated expenses would be to lower both the marginal and the average cost curves discussed in chapter 5 (see figure 5d) by a constant sum per unit of output. Thus the discounted cost curves would lie below and parallel to the original curves [138].

Figure 7d brings together the fire business revenue curves of the small tariff insurance company illustrated in figure 6.1 of chapter 6, and the discounted marginal and average variable cost

Figure 7d

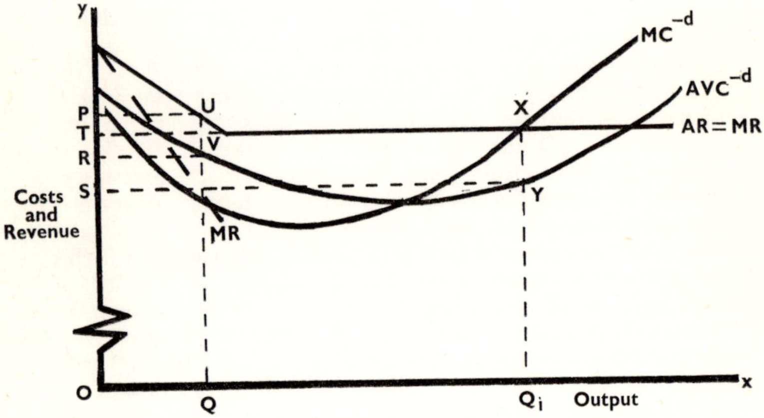

[138]   This is easily proved algebraically. Taking the average variable cost for n units,

$$AVC_n = \frac{TVC_n}{n}$$

and breaking down total variable cost into its component parts so that

$$TVC_n = nC + E_n,$$

then

$$AVC_n = \frac{nC + E_n}{n}$$

where C = expected claims cost per unit of output (measured as a standard unit of loss expectancy) plus associated claims expenses

E_n = the sum of the other variable costs

As C is constant, the average investment income per unit of output will also be a constant k, so that the discounted average variable cost will be

$$AVC_n - d\frac{n(C-k) + E_n}{n}$$

continued on page 123

curves MC^{-d} and AVC^{-d} [139]. It can be seen that the marginal cost curve cuts the marginal revenue curve twice—at output OQ where marginal revenue and marginal cost are falling, and at output OQ_1 where marginal revenue is equal to average revenue. Should the company follow the tariff price OT, or charge the higher premium rate level OP and accept the reduction in the volume of business? The contribution to fixed costs to be gained from charging the tariff rate is equal to the rectangle STXY; at the price OP it falls to PUVR, so given the cost curves shown the company would be better advised to conform to the tariff.

Given little scope for charging above the tariff rates and the relatively flat marginal cost curve this result is not entirely surprising. On the other hand would the company gain any advantage by leaving the tariff organisation and charging lower premium rates? Unless at the same time it could secure a relatively greater reduction in its costs there would be no short-run advantage to be gained by doing so. At the tariff rate it is able to sell as much insurance as it desires given its existing capacity, and if, for example, it cut price to OR it would be necessary also to cut output in order to keep marginal cost equal to marginal revenue, so that total revenue would fall. However, with the average variable cost curve being flatter than the MC^{-d} curve, the reduction in average variable costs would fall less than total revenue thereby reducing the contribution towards fixed costs. It may be added that in practice a company which left the F.O.C. also initially may risk losing a substantial volume of business through the operation of the 65/35 per cent rule mentioned on page 110 because it would not be able to retain an interest in any large fire insurances where previously its share had been sufficient to give tariff companies only a bare 65 per cent of the total schedule.

If this analysis accurately reflects the real life position of small fire insurers (and it is significant that not only were many of the smaller companies apparently reluctant to see the ending of the

---

[138] *continued from page* 122

$$= \frac{nC - nk + E_n}{n}$$

$$\text{and } AVC_n{}^{-d} - AVC_n = \frac{-nk}{n} = -k$$

Thus at each output the discounted average variable cost will be equal to AVC less the value of the constant discount factor.

The reader is left to provide a similar proof for marginal cost.

[139] In order to make the diagram easier to read the vertical scale has been increased, so making the U-shaped cost curves steeper than in figure 6.1.

motor tariff[140], but also there have been very few resignations from the F.O.C.), it is reasonable to ask why new companies invariably enter the market as non-tariff insurers. Ignoring any restrictions which the Fire Offices' Committee may place on membership, a new company may decide that independence of action offers the better chance of long-run success than does adherence to the association's rules. Three reasons may be given for such a view:

(a) that by remaining independent the company can reduce costs; for example, a company can avoid the costs of membership, including the cost of analysing loss data required by the Committee, and still fairly easily obtain details of tariff rates. Exactly what this means in terms of actual costs is not publicly known, but could represent a significant saving.

(b) it may take a longer-term view and decide that independence of action may offer better opportunities for more rapid growth which would enable it to secure the cost advantages of any available economies of scale. In other words, it may be prepared to sacrifice immediate profits for better long-term prospects.

(c) besides obtaining freedom of pricing, the company would be free to offer higher commissions to brokers. This could have two possible benefits. It may enable the company to attract business from a wider geographical area without incurring the substantial costs of establishing branch offices. Secondly an increase in brokers' commissions may be more effective in stimulating demand than premium reductions of an equivalent size; in other words, it may prove possible to attract a much larger volume of business at a smaller loss of net revenue per unit of output than would be possible by direct price competition[141]. Again, these two effects are important in relation to long-run expansion.

If we now look at the position of the large tariff company its pricing strategy may be considered in the short and long run. In the short run, given its existing underwriting capacity, its pricing policy will depend upon whether it can obtain as much business as it desires at the going tariff rates without being left with spare capacity. Being larger than the small company it may have been able to exploit some economies of scale so that at capacity level it may enjoy lower unit costs, and therefore be able to secure larger profits in both absolute and relative terms.

On the other hand, if by operating at tariff rates the company is faced with problems of spare capacity it will need to reconsider its continuing membership of the tariff association. Such a decision has implications for both short- and long-run profitability

---

140 see p 13 above.
141 This could be a key factor. It will be recalled that the Equity and Law resigned from the Life Offices' Association to meet the competition from non-member companies which had used more generous commission terms as a means of securing support from brokers (see page 12). Subsequently two small companies also resigned but the constraints on life offices leaving their association are nothing like so severe as those facing fire insurance companies.

throughout the industry; the departure of a major company from a tariff association would substantially disturb overall market conditions, calling into question the continuance of the price fixing agreement and the pricing policies of existing independent insurers. In other words, the company could not regard its actions as being independent of the rest of the market.

The events following the breakdown of the Accident Offices' Association's motor tariff in 1969 would provide an excellent subject for research into the interdependence of major companies in the market and the interactions resulting from independent attempts to secure larger market shares. The freedom of action previously enjoyed by non-tariff insurers had enabled them to secure an increasingly larger share of the market and of the better quality risks, so forcing the tariff companies periodically to retaliate, but every re-adjustment of the tariff rates had been countered by new moves from the more aggressive independent companies. After the ending of the tariff most of the major ex-tariff companies sought to attract extra business by introducing new rating plans providing lower premiums for selected groups of motorists. Although such action may have proved successful from the standpoint of the amount of business the companies were able to regain from their erstwhile non-tariff competitors, the immediate cost in terms of larger underwriting losses throughout the market was high. Amongst the sufferers were the ex-independent companies and Lloyd's syndicates. The new competition from old tariff companies coincided with a period of rapid inflation which seriously affected claims and expense costs, and the next two years saw the failure of several companies, including the Vehicle and General, whose earlier successes had contributed to the abandonment of the tariff.

It is not clear whether the decision to abandon the tariff was taken primarily to improve profitability or to restore earlier market shares. Though the result was an immediate deterioration in profits this is not necessarily inconsistent with long-run profit maximisation. Certainly the demise of the tariff has changed market conditions. There no longer exists a standard schedule of tariff premiums which the more conventional independent companies can simply cut by a small percentage, leaving aggressive insurers to exploit any weaknesses in the classification system in the safe knowledge that the inevitable delays involved in securing the agreement of all members will protect them from swift retaliation by tariff companies.

All forms of collective price agreements tend to be unstable but agreements in the insurance markets are subject to a particular weakness. The calculation of schedule premium rates first calls for agreement on group classifications; while broadly defined rating groups have statistical advantages they also introduce the risk of lack of homogeneity through the inclusion in one rating class of different groups of individuals with significantly different loss expectancies. The threat such a situation poses to the tariff system is illustrated in figure 7e: it is assumed that included in the tariff rating class X are two groups A and B with loss expectancies of £30 and £20 respectively and the tariff premium is based on a combined loss expectancy of £25. If an independent insurer is able to identify the two groups it may attract the business of group B by offering a premium rate lower than the tariff, so leaving the tariff companies with group A.

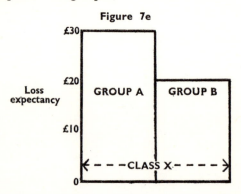

Figure 7e

Under such conditions tariff companies may find themselves not only with a declining share of the market and consequent spare capacity, but also the business they retain carries an inadequate premium rate. Obviously this was the situation from which the major tariff companies sought to escape when they abandoned the motor tariff and were prepared to accept the risks of a short-lived price war before a new (and hopefully more profitable for them) market equilibrium was achieved.

So to return to the problem of the large tariff company, it knows that every conceivable course of action carries certain risks, and that any attempts at independent action designed to secure larger profits and/or a larger share of the market is almost certain to incite retaliatory action from competitors. Moreover present market structure is such that no company is sufficiently powerful to be able to dominate the market; all face competition from other companies equally capable of matching their actions. What it does not know for certain is the extent of such retaliation.

A unilateral decision to leave the F.O.C. in order to pursue an independent pricing policy would have more serious implications than the abandonment of the motor tariff. The first problem would be the rearrangement of the insurances in which the company had a part-share, possibly involving the company in a certain immediate loss of business. Secondly the problems of rate-making on sound statistical grounds are far more difficult than for motor insurance because of the smaller loss frequencies and, for many classes of risk, the limited number of exposure units, both of which necessitate the pooling of experience by a large section of the market in order to produce creditable statistics. (It is noteworthy that the companies have chosen to abandon only the household tariff where a major company insuring a large number of houses can have considerable confidence in its own experience, particularly as such risks are not subject to the same rate of change as many industrial fire risks which are exposed to the influence of changes in manufacturing processes, the introduction of new materials, etc.) Under such conditions the expected increase in profits would need to be large to induce a major company to leave the tariff organisation, and at a time like the present when rising fire losses continue quickly to overtake agreed increases in premium rates, so that insurers find it extremely difficult to earn even marginal underwriting profits and the market suffers from a shortage of capacity, not surprisingly there is no sign of any companies contemplating the possibility of leaving the Fire Offices' Committee.

If, on the other hand, in a period of market prosperity a large company found itself with spare capacity, while independent insurers were gaining an increasing share of the market, then the temptation to cut tariff premium rates would be greater. One possible approach to the problem then would be to examine the expected outcome of alternative courses of action.

The company would start from a known position with definite information regarding its present output, level of variable costs, premium and investment income, and, therefore, the contribution fire business makes to its fixed costs. Looking ahead it also ought to be able to make fairly reliable estimates of the management expenses it would incur at different levels of output and likewise its expected claims costs (subject to the same degree of variation in actual claims results as it experiences on its present level of business). The major area of uncertainty would be in relation to expected demand at different premium rate levels, for a great deal would depend on the reaction of competitors. Clearly the likelihood of the company being able to increase substantially its premium income, and perhaps its profits too, by cutting its premium rates would be higher if no other company left the tariff association, but faced with the loss of business to the former member would this be likely? It must be assumed that competitors are as intelligent as oneself so that the company must consider two possible outcomes of its action, which are illustrated in diagram 7f, (see page 128).

The company's current level of premium rates (i.e. the tariff rates) and output are given by point C. Curve DD is based on the assumption that other tariff companies would not follow any change in premium rates made by the company, whereas curve

128

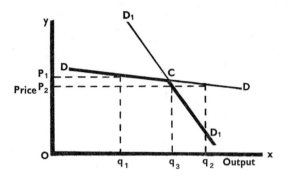

D_1D_1 shows the position if other companies did react accordingly. Given the assumptions of profitable underwriting operations but with spare capacity in the tariff sector of the market, it is unlikely that other companies would follow an increase in premium rates, so that an attempt to raise rates to OP_1 would result in a substantial cut in output to Oq_1 [142]. Conversely a reduction in premium rates to OP_2 could have two possible results: if other companies did not retaliate the company may enjoy a substantial increase in business to Oq_2 whereas if other major companies followed the cut in premiums the gain could be as small as Oq_3. (Readers may notice that the thickly drawn curve DCD_1 is the kinked demand curve mentioned in chapter 6 when dealing with the position of large independent companies). Thus the company may conclude that its demand curve would be relatively elastic if it attempted to raise its premium rates but relatively inelastic for a cut in rates. If correct this would mean that any change in rates would result in in a loss of premium income, a risk which the company may not be prepared to take, especially in a market situation where it is far more difficult to reverse a price reduction.

On the other hand there is a chance that other companies may not retaliate, in which case a change of premium rates may yield higher profits. In an attempt to maximise profits should the company accept the risk of loss of present profits? One approach to solving this problem is to examine the likely effect of these various possibilities on the size of the contribution fire business makes to fixed costs and profits, as follows.

Taking a hypothetical example, let us assume that the com-

---

[142] A unilateral decision to increase premium rates would not necessitate resignation from the F.O.C., which specifies *minimum* rates.

pany's present position is as given below:

Fire Premium income	£25·0 million
Discounted variable costs	£22·5

Contribution to fixed costs £2·5 million
and profit

Using the estimates it has made of its variable costs (i.e. claims, reinsurance, sales and management costs) at various levels of output, and discounting them at an appropriate rate of interest as explained above, the company then could calculate the contributions it would expect to earn at different premium rate levels (a) assuming that other companies do not follow its lead, and (b) on the assumption that they do retaliate, setting out the results as in columns 2a and 3a of table 7.1 (page 130) [143]. For the sake of simplicity no attempt has been made to distinguish between degrees of retaliation although in real life competitors may decide either completely or only partially to match price changes.

The next step for the company would be to try to attach probability ratings to the potential reactions of major competitors to the various possible changes in its premium rates; e.g. what would be the probability that competitors would ignore a 5 per cent premium reduction? In this task the company would be guided by its knowledge of the industry, and in particular of the current state of opinion and standards of management amongst its competitors. As it has been assumed that for each change of premium rates its competitors could adopt only two possible courses of action—to ignore the change or to retaliate—the sum of the two probabilities shown in columns 2b and 3b must be equal to 1(=certainty).

The expected value of each event shown in columns 2c and 3c is then calculated by multiplying the expected contribution by its probability rating, and the total expected value of each of the possible changes in premium rates is given by adding together the two individual values so that in column 4 the combined expected values of the various premium changes under consideration can be compared.

The table indicates that, at least so far as short-run profitability is concerned, the company would be better off remaining a tariff member because its present contribution from fire business to its fixed costs (£2·5 million) is larger than any of the alternative total expected values shown in column 4. Looking at some of the individual expected results, it was assumed that if other major

---

[143] To avoid misunderstanding it must be emphasised that though every endeavour has been made to produce a realistic example, the table is purely intended to be illustrative of the principles involved. Both the results shown and the underlying calculations are based on purely hypothetical figures, and do not relate to the known experience of any actual company.

Table 7.1 (see page 129)

Expected values of contributions to fixed costs and profits produced by premium rate changes

Row	Column 1 Percentage change in premium rates	Column 2 Competitors not retaliating			Column 3 Competitors retaliating			Column 4
		(a) Contribution £m	(b) × Probability =	(c) Expected value £m	(a) Contribution £m	(b) × Probability =	(c) Expected value £m	Total Expected value £m
i	+10%	1·25	0·90	1·13	4·52	0·10	0·45	1·58
ii	+5%	2·02	0·90	1·82	4·15	0·10	0·41	2·23
iii	−5%	3·90	0·25	0·98	1·10	0·75	0·83	1·81
iv	−10%	1·20	0·25	0·30	0·50	0·75	0·38	0·68

companies did not retaliate a 10 per cent cut in premium rates would produce a substantially larger increase in the volume of business and so too in premium income, but working on the hypothesis that insurers' variable costs are relatively unresponsive to changes in output so that average variable cost would not fall in proportion to the cut in premium rates, the outcome is a reduction in the net contribution to £1·2 million (see row iv, column 2a). On the other hand, a 5 per cent cut in premium rates (see row iii) which is not followed by competitors is shown as producing an increase in profits, but because the company believes that there is a 75 per cent chance that other major companies would swiftly cut premiums too, so causing its net contribution to fall below the existing level, the combined total expected value of this move is a fall in the net contribution to £1·81 million. The best strategy indicated by the table would be to persuade fellow tariff companies to raise premiums by 10 per cent (see row i, column 3a), but the company believes that there is only a one in ten chance of achieving this, while the expected result of a unilateral increase in premium rates of such magnitude would be a halving of its present contribution [144].

Long-run profit maximisation

If instead of short-run profit maximisation the company sets its sights on the long run the difficulties assume new dimensions. The longer the time horizon the more uncertain become the values of all of the variables involved, and new factors enter into the

---

[144]   Two criticisms may be levelled against this example:

(a)   It incorporates too little detail. Not only does it not allow for differing degrees of retaliation by competitors, but also it ignores the fact that for each possible response by competitors the company may experience several possible outcomes, each of which needs to be examined using conditional probabilities. Also the payback period of any proposed change of premium rates needs to be considered; the longer the time period under review the more important it becomes to treat the cumulative profit outcomes of different price changes in such a way as to place them on a comparable basis (see footnote 145 below). Interested readers can find an example of such an approach to price decision-taking by P. Green in "Bayesian decision theory in pricing strategy", *Journal of Marketing*, 27 January 1963.

(b)   It assumes that the values which companies place on expected profits are proportional to their monetary values. This may not be entirely true. For example, two companies may place different values on a 10 per cent chance of gaining a £500,000 profit compared with a 50 per cent chance of a profit of £100,000, even though the expected values of both events is equal to £50,000. The reason lies in differing attitudes to risk. John S. Hammond has suggested a method of dealing with this problem by calculating certainty equivalents of different outcomes using preference curve analysis: see "Better decisions with preference theory", *Harvard Business Review*, November-December 1967.

problem. The company may feel confident that as it expands its capacity so significant cost economies could be achieved. Thus in the long run the contribution to be achieved from the increase in business produced by a 10 per cent cut in premium rates may be thought to be substantially larger than the figure shown in table 7·1, so that the company may consider it worthwhile to accept a fall in present profits for the sake of higher earnings in later years [145].

Confidence in demand estimates, however, must decline the longer the time horizon under review, although in a growing market an over-estimate for any particular year will tend to be a less serious matter than in a static market. Over time, demand will be affected by the various factors discussed in chapter 6, but in addition note must be taken of the influence of prices (and profits) on the number of potential competitors which may be attracted to the market.

The threat of new entry

As noted in chapter 1, the 1960's saw a substantial rise in new entry to the British insurance market. Logically there are only three reasons why a new firm should seek to enter any market. It may hope to earn higher profits than are obtainable in other industries with the same degree of risk because:

(i) it hopes to be able to participate in high profits being earned by existing firms; or
(ii) using existing methods it believes that it can operate more efficiently than existing firms; or
(iii) it intends to enter as an innovator.

Obviously if established firms pursue a policy of high prices and profits this will act as an open invitation to new firms to enter the market.

In addition to the legal barriers to entry outlined in chapter 1, a study of the British non-life market during the seond half of the 1960's [146] indicated that the obstacles facing a new entrant arise from the following advantages enjoyed by established insurers:

(i) economies of large scale
(ii) absolute cost advantages;
(iii) easier access to and lower costs of reinsurance;
(iv) product differentiation; and
(v) advantages arising from the present market organisation.

---

[145] In effect the company would be investing in future profitability, and in order to decide whether the expected higher profits in future years were sufficient to compensate for the present loss of profit the company could use the investment appraisal technique of discounted cash flow. This involves the discounting of future receipts at an appropriate rate of interest: for example, using a discount rate of 8 per cent estimated extra profits of £100 earned 5 years hence would be equal to present profits of £68 ·06.

[146] R. L. Carter *Competition in the British fire and accident insurance market* chapter III.

It is impossible to examine in detail here all of the factors involved but the following comments provide a brief summary of the main points which a potential entrant would need to consider before making a final decision.

1. Economies of scale constitute a serious obstacle to potential new entrants when minimum optimal scale occurs at a high level of output relative to the size of the market, and costs fall substantially up to that point, particularly if substantial capital investment is necessary in order to achieve such an output. For example, in the situation illustrated in figure 7g average costs fall so sharply that a firm operating substantially below the minimum optimal scale output OA could not hope to compete. If OA

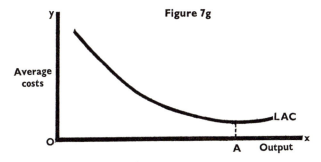

Figure 7g

represented a substantial share of the total market, then in order to survive a new entrant would need to compete away from established firms a significant part of their market shares. Almost certainly this would provoke retaliatory action, although a new entrant may be more fortunate in a rapidly expanding market which could accommodate an increase in total capacity.

On the basis of the analysis of costs in Chapter 5 it may be concluded that, although a new entrant to the insurance industry faces some relatively small disadvantage from this source, it does not constitute an important barrier to entry. The empirical evidence too clearly shows that new entrants (and older established firms) can operate successfully at low levels of output well below the minimum optimal scale level of premium income.

2. Absolute cost advantages are present where established firms enjoy the benefits of lower average costs than could be achieved by even the most favoured potential entrant. There are a number of factors operating in the British fire and accident insurance market which possibly could provide established insurers with such cost advantages *vis-à-vis* new entrants; for example:

(a) capital barriers to entry and the higher cost of capital for the new entrant;
(b) imperfections in the labour market which may impose higher

labour costs on new entrants because of the need to compete away from established companies the necessary qualified staff;

(c) the control by established insurers of the channels of distribution resulting in higher selling costs for new entrants;

(d) established insurers' control of production techniques and access to vital information; and

(e) the availability and cost of reinsurance facilities for new insurers.

Again the evidence demonstrates that these obstacles are surmountable by a new entrant. Indeed, although certain higher costs may be inevitable it may be possible to avoid others borne by major established firms. One possible area of saving was suggested on page 124, and initially it is possible to avoid the cost of a branch office organisation by using brokers to obtain nationwide representation, though the need to offer higher commission rates may offset some of the saving.

3. Reinsurance provides an additional system of risk transfer, enabling insurers to spread further the risk of loss; to improve the stability of their underwriting results; and to achieve greater flexibility in the type and size of risks an insurer is able to accept. The smaller are the premium income, capital and free reserves of an insurance company, the greater is its need for reinsurance protection. Although reinsurance requirements vary considerably for different classes of insurance, access to the reinsurance market is essential for a new entrant[147].

The evidence indicates that a potential new entrant faces two barriers in trying to obtain the reinsurance protection it needs to operate safely. It may not be able to obtain precisely the type of cover it would like; for example, new motor insurers may not be able to obtain quota share reinsurance, so restricting their rate of expansion, and on excess loss covers it may be necessary for a company to carry higher retention limits than desired[148]. Secondly, it will have to pay a larger proportion of its gross premium income for reinsurance than a large established company.

On the other hand the degree of competition which exists in a market as international as reinsurance minimises the disadvantages

---

[147] It will be recalled that proof must be supplied to the Department of Trade and Industry that adequate reinsurance arrangements have been made before authorisation can be granted to commence business. (Section 63, Companies Act, 1967.)

[148] Under a *quota share* reinsurance the reinsurer takes a fixed share of all business accepted by the direct insurance company, paying an equivalent proportion of all claims and receiving in return the same share of total direct premiums less an overriding commission.

Excess loss: the reinsurer accepts liability up to a prescribed limit for any loss in excess of an agreed amount, either in respect of individual claims or the aggregate of all claims arising from a single occurrence. The premium is based primarily upon the direct insurer's past claims experience, and this operates as one source of difficulty in arranging such reinsurance for a new company.

suffered by new companies. A great deal depends on the new entrant itself: a well-founded company with an experienced management which proposes to operate in a conventional manner would be unlikely to encounter any major disadvantage in acquiring the reinsurance protection it required.

4. Product differentiation advantages to established insurers may be identified under a number of headings:

(1) The accumulated preference of buyers for established insurers based on their reputations for financial strength, quality of service provided, etc.; such qualities may be either real or induced by prolonged advertising.

(2) Membership of market associations which generate buyer preference. The advertising campaign conducted by the British Insurance Association following the collapse of several new motor insurers in 1966 and 1967 was a notable attempt to achieve such a result which unfortunately lost much of its credibility following the collapse of the Vehicle and General in 1971.

(3) The local connections and personal contacts built up over many years by established companies, often based on a network of branch offices.

(4) Customer inertia and loyalty to a particular insurer.

A major dilemma for a potential new entrant is that in order to attract broker/public support it must offer some inducement to overcome such product differentiation advantages enjoyed by established companies. The new life insurer at least is in a better position than the new entrant to the non-life market in that the former has ready access to reliable loss statistics in the form of published mortality tables from which it can safely devise new forms of life contract. On the other hand in a market as security conscious as insurance, any departure from the established norms are likely to prolong the period before a new company is considered respectable by the remainder of the market. A major part of the strategy for a company selling personal insurance may be extensive advertising directed at the general public, which generally possesses scant knowledge of the respective merits of the various established insurance companies, with a very few notable exceptions.

5. Market organisation. The major change which has taken place in market organisation over the last 20 years has been the development of provincial brokers which has eased the conditions of entry for new insurers. Again, however, where the new entrant is concentrating on personal insurances it may be worth while investigating the possibilities of by-passing the normal market sales organisation by adopting either direct selling (perhaps mail-order) or seeking a link with a bank, multiple retailer or other organisation able to provide a nationwide sales network.

After studying all of the above factors and the statutory barriers to entry, a well-founded new company may conclude that the overall condition of entry to the British insurance market is relatively easy. In the case of a well-established foreign company this is particularly so. The actual size of the disadvantages which would be encountered would depend on the prospective entrant's proposed scale of operation and classes of business to be undertaken, but there would be no need to attempt entry at a level anywhere approaching optimal scale.

The implications for established insurers of the existence of such conditions are obvious. Even though it may take five or more years before the entry of a new company becomes full effective in the sense of it achieving a secure place in the market and influencing prevailing conditions, established insurers cannot afford to ignore the total, much shorter, effect of several new companies deciding to enter the market together.

To see how these conditions may affect market performance one may turn to the work of Joe S. Bain [149]. Given the dominance of a few large company groups and the general tendency for co-operation between insurers already noted in earlier chapters, the prevailing conditions closely fit Bain's assumptions regarding oligopolies operating in a state of continued ineffectively impeded entry [150]. This situation, he predicted, may eventually through new entry lead to a stable market composed of a large number of firms competing by price. However, this condition will tend to be followed by regroupings through mergers, and because of the small differential advantages possessed by a relatively few established firms, a period of competitive pricing will tend to re-establish their dominanace of the market, reinstate high concentration and set off "another cycle of high, entry-inducing pricing" [151]. Without spending a lot of time on detailed analysis it may be suggested that the performance of the insurance industry in the last decade strongly supports these predictions.

Therefore in deciding on long-run pricing strategy the problem for large established insurers is whether it is more profitable to set prices and profit targets at levels sufficiently low to discourage potential new entrants, or whether it is better to accept the risks and discomforts of short-run profit maximising, seizing opportunities for high profits whenever they occur.

Full cost pricing

Viewed in the context of insurance literature from both sides of the Atlantic, the foregoing discussion of profit maximisation may seem far removed from actual practice in the industry. The general assumption is that insurers fix their premium rates in relation to expected claims costs, adding an allowance for expenses and profit.

---

[149] *Barriers to new competition,* Harvard University Press (1956)
[150] *ibid,* p33
[151] *ibid,* p36

Thus the basic premium equation usually is expressed in the following form:

$$P = q \times \bar{c} + (E + y)$$

where
$P =$ premium
$q =$ probability of a loss occurring
$\bar{c} =$ the average amount payable on the happening of the event
$E =$ loading for expenses
$y =$ loading for profit

$$P = E + y + (q \times \bar{c})$$

In the case of certain classes of business it is well recognised that the equation needs to be modified for time lags in the payment of premiums and/or claims, so introducing an interest element. The most important of these is life business for which the basic equation can be adjusted as follows for a proprietary company transacting non-profit business:

$$\Sigma \left\{ P_t - E_t - q_t C_t \right\} (1 + i)^{-t} = y \quad [152]$$

To allow for the fact that all of the items are payable over a period of years (indicated by the suffix t) they are discounted at a rate of interest i, equivalent to the rate which the company conservatively assumes that it will be able to earn by investing its life funds. However, as noted already, generally insurers argue that similar allowance for investment earnings should not be brought into account when calculating non-life premiums.

Despite all of the efforts now being made to improve forecasts of expected costs and investment earnings some uncertainty inevitably remains in the eventual profit results. Indeed it is this uncertainty which frequently is advanced for employing a full-cost pricing convention, and for the formation of tariff associations, which can restrain the over-optimistic. Also there is a feeling that the system is fair to the consumer in that the insurer looks only for a "reasonable" rate of profit on the business and each group of policyholders is expected to pay a premium closely related to the costs transferred to the insurer. The latter argument is consistent with a traditional and widely held belief in the industry that its principal objective is to serve the public [153].

---

[152] This is an equation developed by W. E. Beard in "Some Thoughts on the Solvency of Insurance Companies", Jubilee number of the Quarterly letter of the Algemeene Reinsurance Companies. Vol. 1. July 1964.

[153] In the discussion on the CII Conference paper "Insurance profitability past, present and future", D. F. Dunstan was reported as saying, "We were all sincere in our belief that one of our functions as insurance people was to provide a proper service to the community at large". *Journal* of Chartered Insurance Institute, Vol. 66 (1969) p157.

138

Consideration of the public interest is laudable, but it can be demonstrated that full-cost pricing in its most naive form may serve neither the interest of the public nor shareholders. Obviously long-run survival at a time of rising costs (whether as the result of changing risk factors or inflation) depends on using prospective rather than past costs as the premium base; also in calculating the loading for expenses a view must be taken of the anticipated level of business which will be transacted. Even with these refinements full-cost pricing ignores demand and the forces of competition. Consequently the final profit outcome will be rather more fortuitous than the result of good judgment.

For example, in figure 7h it is assumed that the premium rate level is fixed at OP_F on a full-cost basis. With demand at the level given by curve AR_1 (with the corresponding curve MR_1) this is below the profit maximising rate level OP_1, but if demand fell to AR_2 the full-cost rate would be above the profit maximising level OP_2. If the objective was to make the most efficient use of

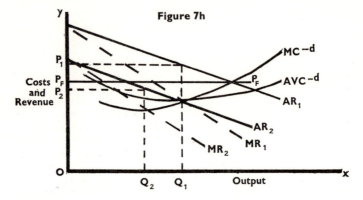

insurance services in the public interest then it could be argued that this would be best served by charging a premium rate which would equate marginal cost and average revenue.

In reality many insurers probably do pay some regard to demand and the state of competition in the market, adjusting the expense/profit loading accordingly[154]. Also there is evidence that the major companies consider the influence of premium changes for non-life business on investment income, even if they do not yet go to the point of building it into their actual calculations. Nevertheless it is suggested that better results would be achieved, whether the objective is to maximise profits or to serve the public,

[154] See, for example, D. I. W. Reynolds *Motor insurance rate fixing,* Institute of Actuaries Students Society 1970. Reynolds shows that an optimal pricing policy must pay regard to possible gains and losses of business when considering a premium rating change.

by paying more regard to marginal (discounted) costs and demand estimates, in order to evaluate the effect of different rates of premium on the net contribution each class of business could make to fixed costs and profit, than by adhering to a rating convention which pays inadequate consideration to demand and relies on what in part can be only an arbitrary allocation of expenses between different classes of business.

Sales maximisation

Before leaving pricing a brief mention must be made of the maximisation of premium income which may appear to be a desirable objective for an insurer.

Ignoring the possibility of obtaining cost reductions through economies of scale, sales maximisation may appear desirable to insurers for various reasons. W. J. Baumol has suggested that for the sake of their own prestige and salary prospects managements of large firms will choose to increase sales rather than profits, subject to the constraint of needing to earn some minimum level of profit sufficient to keep shareholders satisfied[155].

This situation is illustrated in figure 7i: total profit is maximised at output OQ_1 while total sales (i.e. revenue) are maximised at output OQ_2. If the firm was satisfied with a profit level OR_1 then sales maximisation would yield more than the prescribed minimum profit. If, however, the firm fixed a minimum profit level of OR_2 it would act as a constraint on the growth of sales.

Figure 7i

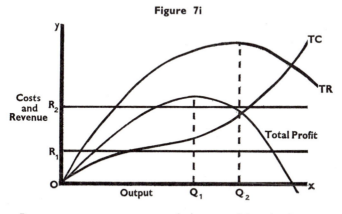

Insurance management may be attracted by the investment opportunities generated by the growth of premium income, and indeed see it as a means of increasing profits. The advantage for the life office is the scope offered for the employment of specialist investment staff, and participation in more highly specialised

[155] W. J. Baumol *Business behaviour, value and growth*, Macmillan (1959).

forms of investment, e.g. property, Whether this produces a significant improvement in investment performance would make an interesting research subject.

Non-life managements traditionally have tended to view underwriting performance in terms of underwriting results, i.e. net premium income less claims and expenses, treating investment earnings as an additional contribution towards reserves, and dividends. As noted above, investment earnings also have been excluded from premium calculations. Consequently there is the temptation to regard investment earnings as a separate source of income which can be increased by expanding premium income, thereby increasing overall profits. While the former assumption is correct, the latter does not necessarily follow. It has been shown already that in order to expand output a company facing a downward sloping demand curve must be prepared to cut price. Thus unless marginal cost is less than marginal revenue, the result of cutting premium rates in order to expand premium income would be a fall in underwriting profits which may well be larger than the increase in investment income. As demonstrated above, if the aim is to maximise profits the only way to approach the problem is through full information regarding marginal costs and revenue, including investment earnings, and under certain conditions profit maximisation may call for measures which will produce a fall in premium income. Sales maximisation and profit maximisation should never be treated as identical objectives.

THE PERFORMANCE OF INSURERS

Exactly how one measures the performance of an insurance company depends partly on one's point of view, whether it be that of a shareholder, policyholder, employee, or general member of the public, all of whom to some degree have differing interests. Therefore, in evaluating the performance of any company the first task is to decide upon the main objective(s) of the group concerned, but even then either the ends, or the means by which they may be achieved, may prove to be mutually incompatible in either the short or the long run. For example, the desire by policyholders for low stable premium rates in non-life insurance may conflict with an equally desirable rapid expansion of insurers' capacity during a period of inflation.

Such difficulties in judging company performance are not unique to the insurance industry. Under the provisions of the Monopolies and Restrictive Practices (Inquiry and Control) Act 1948 the Monopolies Commission is required to examine whether industries referred to it are operating in the public interest. The Act itself merely lists a number of criteria against which performance is to be judged, leaving the Commission to decide on balance in each case whether the firm or industry is, or is not, acting in the public interest.

Using the same broad test of the public interest and recognising that the basic function of insurance is the transfer of risks, the principal question to be asked about the insurance industry is whether it provides the public with adequate facilities for the transfer of those risks which cannot be handled more economically by other methods, at fair premiums correctly related to the risks transferred, and with a guarantee that claims will be settled fairly and promptly [156]. In the case of life business this proposed standard of performance may need to be extended. The bulk of the business now handled by life offices contains a large savings element so that the policyholder is concerned not only with the transfer of risk but also the rate of return he will obtain on his savings; likewise the public is interested in the manner in which the life offices invest their funds. As explained in Chapter 4, given the imperfections of the capital market and the differing degrees of risk associated with different types of investment, it is difficult to formulate a precise measure of investment performance, though, subject to qualifications regarding risk, a rate of return embracing both income and capital gains offers the best practical measure.

Taking the above definitions of the public interest as the appropriate standards of desirable behaviour for insurers, the following measures of performance suggest themselves:

(1) whether insurers are producing and distributing their services efficiently;
(2) the level of prices (i.e. premiums) prevailing in relation to costs;
(3) whether premiums are fairly discriminatory between different groups of policyholders;
(4) the levels of profit attained in the industry;
(5) whether new forms of cover are made available promptly when the need arises;
(6) whether market capacity keeps abreast of demand;
(7) whether insurers have sufficient resources to meet all liabilities, present and prospective;

And in relation to life business:

(8) how efficiently insurers utilise the funds at their disposal, and
(9) whether profits, including capital gains, are fairly distributed between different generations of with-profit policyholders.

Amongst these measures of performance, efficiency and profitability are the subject of annual studies by both stockbrokers, and the financial and insurance press [157]. Occasionally other studies are

---

[156] Such an interpretation of the public interest accords with the simple definition employed by Jack Downie who said that the public interest is "What the public is interested in", *The Competitive Process*, p30 Duckworth & Co. (1958).

[157] For British companies see the annual surveys privately circulated by stockbrokers W. Greenwell & Co., and Read Hurst Brown & Co. Annually the *Economist* publishes an insurance supplement and the *Policy Holder Insurance Journal* publishes a survey of the 10 leading composite companies. The American market is well served by *Best's Insurance Services*.

published providing longer term analyses of performance covering a wider range of subjects [158]. Every attempt to measure performance, however, runs into major conceptual and practical problems. Many of the measures are difficult to define in a manner which is both theoretically sound and will receive a large measure of agreement throughout the industry: the problem of the treatment of capital gains, realised and unrealised, in the measurement of profitability may be mentioned as one example of the conceptual problems encountered with non-life business. Unfortunately the conventional measures accepted in the industry often are far from satisfactory.

The major practical problem is the lack of data. Despite the ever-increasing wealth of detail provided in accounts and annual returns prepared for the regulatory authorities, available published information remains insufficient for completely accurate comparative analysis of the performance of companies, which differ in types of business transacted and geographical areas of operation. Indeed the evidence shows that even the regulatory authorities with access to internal information encounter difficulties in evaluating the solvency of insurers, as was demonstrated by the failure of the Vehicle & General where the company's under-estimation of outstanding claims had had the dual effect of under-valuing its liabilities and of inflating its disclosed profits. Almost 25 years ago Professor S. J. Lengyel described the shortcomings of insurance company accounts, and though some progress has been made to improve the quantity and quality of the information made available to the public, much of his critical analysis still remains valid [159]. Part of the difficulty lies in dispensations enjoyed by insurance companies under the provisions of the Companies Acts and in particular from the freedom granted to show assets at book values, provided that in the aggregate such values are not less than current market values, so enabling the accumulation of hidden reserves.

Any investigation of the measures of performance which cannot be evaluated by an analysis of financial data inevitably runs into even more difficulties. Available evidence often is at no more than an anecdotal level, difficult to substantiate, fragmentary and often conflicting. For example, complaints from large buyers of insur-

---

[158] See, for example, J. Plymen & S. Pullan "Insurance profitability past, present and future" *Journal* of the Chartered Insurance Institute vol. 66 (1969) and for the American market "Prices and profits in the property and liability insurance industry", a report prepared by Arthur D. Little Inc. for the American Insurance Association (1967).
The problems in assessing non-life premiums from the standpoint of fair discrimination have been discussed by C. A. Williams in *Price discrimination in property and liability insurance*. The University of Minnesota Press (1959).

[159] *Insurance accounts: an economic interpretation and analysis*, F. W. Cheshire Pty Ltd. (1947).

ance regarding lack of capacity in the non-life markets often have been countered by assertions that the problem lies not in a lack of capacity but the unwillingness of insurers to cover large risks at inadequate premium rates. It is almost impossible to obtain the evidence necessary to judge which view is correct.

Having broadly indicated the types of problems involved it is now proposed to concentrate on the first measure. Efficiency is at one and the same time both a simple and a complex concept: in its simplest terms it refers to the relationship between the employment of available resources (inputs) and the output of goods and services which the public most desires. Therefore, the measurement of business efficiency must be concerned with two factors. First, whether the firm is using its available resources in such a manner as to minimise the cost of producing its desired output. This means that when management is deciding upon the method of production to use it must consider not only the technological factors but also the relative costs of the various factors of production that will be needed (see pages 68-69 above). Secondly, from amongst the various alternative ways it can use its resources, has the firm chosen to produce those goods and services which provide the greatest satisfaction to society? In a market economy these views of efficiency introduce questions of consumer preferences and the prices of resources and products. Therefore, the criterion of business efficiency is often taken to be the difference between costs incurred and revenue earned, i.e. profit, though this would only ensure the optimum allocation of resources in a perfectly competitive economy[160].

In trying to evaluate the efficiency of insurers there is the difficulty of defining insurance service, which cannot be regarded as limited to accepting the transfer of risks. It must also take account of the provisions made for the public to place their insurances and negotiate claims locally, the scope and quality of the advice available to anyone seeking the best method of handling his risks, how promptly and fairly insurers deal with all of these matters, and in the case of non-life insurers, the loss prevention services they provide. Insurance companies traditionally have placed considerable emphasis on such service though today there is a growing awareness that some members of the public may be prepared to forgo some of the convenience in return for lower premiums, as is evidenced by the General Accident group's DC private motor insurance scheme where the policyholder deals direct with the head office. It is desirable that any measure of efficiency used should allow for variations between insurers in the range and quality of service provided.

---

[160] For a fuller discussion of technical and economic efficiency and welfare optimisation see H. J. Richardson *Economic theory*, Hutchinson (1964).

Measuring efficiency. Three possible avenues of enquiry for examining efficiency are:

(1) the dispersion of efficiency between different insurers;

(2) whether the industry on average is becoming more or less efficient; and

(3) more fundamentally, whether the average output/input ratio is as high as possible, or whether there are organisational or other factors present in the industry preventing the achievement of optimum efficiency.

The measure normally employed within the industry is the commission/expense ratio, However, besides the shortcomings discussed in chapter 5 the ratio also ignores capital employed. There may be an argument for omitting capital employed on the grounds that a substantial part of the capital provided by shareholders remains available for investment, but in view of the wide variation in capital/output ratios shown in table 7.2, to ignore this factor would produce an inadequate measure of the dispersion of efficiency between insurers. The only merit of the crude commission/expense ratio is that it is readily calculated from published

Table 7.2

Capital/output ratios of 30 leading non-life UK insurance companies during 1965

Ratio	Number of companies
under 0·20	3
0·20—0·299	4
0·30—0·399	7
0·40—0·499	8
0·50—0·599	0
0·60—0·799	4
0·80—0·999	1
1·00—1·199	3

Source: Companies Returns under the Insurance Companies Act 1958.

Notes:

(i) The ratios are based on accounts for years ending in the last quarter of 1965 or the first quarter 1966.

(ii) Output is net non-life premium income.

(iii) Capital is represented by free assets calculated in accordance with s.13 Insurance Companies Act 1958.

accounts and the data is available for many years so that it provides a rough check both on progress within the industry and a comparison with performance in other markets abroad.

Table 7.3, for example, sets out the performance of the ten leading non-life companies over a period of four years. It can be seen that the trend was for costs to fall relative to premiums, so suggesting a general improvement in efficiency. However various factors were operating during the period which could have influenced the expense ratios, such as increases in premium rates and changes in the composition of the business underwritten, besides the effects on inflation and the imposition of Selective

Table 7.3

Commission and expenses as a percentage of written fire and accident premiums

Company	1967	1968	1969	1970	Change 1967—1970
	%	%	%	%	%
Royal	34·9	34·4	34·2	33·6	−1·3
Commercial Union	35·5	35·1	34·7	33·6	−1·9
General Accident	33·9	34·3	34·8	33·8	−0·1
Guardian Royal Exchange	37·6	36·1	35·1	33·9	−3·7
Sun Alliance & London	38·2	36·6	37·0	36·0	−2·2
Phoenix	38·6	35·8	35·1	32·9	−5·7
Eagle Star	35·0	35·0	35·7	35·1	+0·1
Norwich Union	37·3	36·3	35·4	34·5	−2·8
Prudential	39·3	38·6	36·5	37·6	−1·7
Co-operative	37·1	36·5	37·8	36·6	−0·5

Note: Companies arranged in descending order of size of general premium income.

Source: Compiled from companies' published accounts.

Employment Tax on the costs of resources employed. Therefore more information would be necessary in order to reach firm conclusions about either overall progress or the comparative performance of individual companies.

An alternative approach to evaluating the dispersion of efficiency between non-life insurers would be to employ a formula developed by Jack Downie, which measures output by means of turnover; includes capital employed; and utilises profitability as a combined measure of production and market efficiency[161]. As adapted for insurers the formula is as follows:

Index 1

$$E_1 = 1 - \beta (r - \bar{r})$$

where

$$\beta = \frac{\text{capital employed}}{\text{net premium income}} \text{ for the firm;}$$

r = the rate of profit for the firm (i.e. profit/capital employed) expressed as a decimal percentage

$\bar{r}$ = the mean rate of profit for the industry.

The smaller is E, the greater the efficiency of the individual insurer relative to the industry as a whole.

Two further terms requiring definition are profit and capital employed. Profit may be taken as either transfers from the revenue accounts (i.e. underwriting profits), or operating profits (i.e. underwriting profit plus investment income less expenses not charged to the underwriting accounts). Here it is more appropriate to employ underwriting profit in order to establish efficiency variations between insurers in the conduct of their main function.

The capital resources at the disposal of a non-life insurer consist of share capital plus free reserves (= shareholders' funds), and the funds available to cover liabilities to policyholders (i.e.

---

[161] *The competitive process, op cit.*

provisions for unearned premiums and outstanding claims = policyholders' funds). Both funds are available for investment, but for the purpose of assessing underwriting efficiency the major distinction is that the shareholders' funds provide the capital base necessary for the conduct of insurance business whereas the policyholders' funds are accumulated in the course of such business. Therefore, for present purposes shareholders' funds are the better measure of capital employed. Further justification for this lies in the varying characteristics of different classes of non-life business, particularly in the average length of claims settlement periods, so that the ratios of policyholders' funds to premium income varies significantly. To include policyholders' funds in the definition of capital employed would, therefore, penalise companies with a more than average proportion of business with relatively long outstanding liabilities to policyholders.

Having carefully defined the various terms in the formula it is essential to recognise its limitations. Three of the more important possible criticisms are as follows:

(1) By using profits as a measure of efficiency the results cannot be compared with those for other industries because of differing market conditions, but the formula does show how efficiently different firms operating in the same markets and with the same opportunities use the resources at their disposal.

(2) Until such time as all insurers reveal the full market values of their assets, some unknown part of the differences in efficiency it reveals between insurers may be attributable to variations in the relative sizes of hidden reserves.

(3) The most serious criticism of the index, however, is its failure to reveal the key relationships between claims, management expenses and premium income. So two companies with identical profits, shareholders' funds and net premium incomes would show the same indices of efficiency even though one was incurring substantially larger management and sales expenses and returning a significantly smaller proportion of premiums to policyholders in the form of claims payments than the other. If the product mix of both companies was the same, the second company should be judged the more efficient from the standpoint of the public interest, but this would not emerge from the index.

In order to deal with the third point and to reveal more clearly the relationship between an insurer's inputs and underwriting output the simplest solution is to use another index based on the conventional index of expenses/premium income which is loaded to include the cost of capital employed. An appropriate view of the cost of capital would be its opportunity cost based on the return which could be obtained from its investment in the capital market, taking the current yield on gilt-edged securities as an apt figure. The amended expenses ratio therefore would be:

$$\frac{e + k}{s} ;$$

and for the purpose of measuring the dispersion of efficiency between companies the index would be calculated as follows:

Index 2

$$E_{11} = 1 + \left(\frac{e + k}{s} - \frac{\bar{e} + \bar{k}}{\bar{s}}\right)$$

where
- e = management expenses + commissions for the firm
- k = cost of capital employed by the firm (shareholders' capital × current redemption yield on gilt-edged securities)
- s = written net premiums of the firm
- $\bar{e}, \bar{k}, \bar{s}$ = equivalent data for the industry.

In order to deal with variations between companies attributable to differences in classes of business underwritten, areas of operation, etc, each insurer's data could be standardised. Taking a hypothetical example, in table 7.4 Company A exactly matches the average efficiency of the industry for both classes of business transacted, but because it underwrites a larger proportion of motor business which incurs relatively lower costs, from its overall results it appears more efficient than the industry in general.

Table 7.4

	Company A			Industry		
	s	$e+k$	$\dfrac{e+k}{s}$	$\bar{s}$	$\bar{e}+\bar{k}$	$\dfrac{\bar{e}+\bar{k}}{\bar{s}}$
	£m	£m		£m	£m	
Fire	5	2·25	0·45	100	45	0·45
Motor	15	4·50	0·30	150	45	0·30
Total	20	6·75	0·338	250	90	0·36

This may be corrected by multiplying Company A's individual expense ratios by the proportions which each class of business bears to the total business transacted by the industry as a whole, as follows:

(a) proportions of fire and motor business underwritten by the industry—

$$\text{Fire} = \frac{100}{250} = 0\cdot 40$$

$$\text{Motor} = \frac{150}{250} = 0\cdot 60$$

(b) standardised result for Company A—

Fire	= 0·45 × 0·40	= 0·18
Motor	= 0·30 × 0·60	= 0·18
Total		0·36

Although the standardising process would make possible comparisons of insurers transacting very different classes of business, the differences between life and general business are such that it would be more satisfactory to analyse them separately. Also when used for life business the standardising process would need to be employed to allow for differences between life and pensions business, and individual and group schemes.

A final qualification is that this second index would not allow for variations in the results between insurers due to differences in the types and standards of service provided, and it is difficult to see how this could be corrected. The only mitigating factor is that companies should be able to offset the higher costs of a superior service by charging higher premium rates which thereby would reduce, though not eliminate, the net effect on the expense ratio.

Turning from the pure underwriting function, the other aspect of the efficiency of an insurer, whether life or general, is the manner in which it employs the funds at its disposal. One possible measure of financial efficiency would be provided by the following formula, where again the smaller is E_{111} the greater is the firm's relative efficiency within the industry:

Index 3

$$E_{111} = 1 - (i - \bar{i})$$

where i = investment yield for the firm (i.e. investment earnings/capital employed).

$\bar{i}$ = mean investment yield for the industry weighted according to capital employed

capital employed = shareholders' funds + policyholders' funds.

The index differs in two important respects from the normal calculations of investment yield employed in the industry:

(a) the definition of capital employed is not restricted to invested funds, thereby extending the index to embrace wider aspects of financial management than the efficiency of investment operations alone. So, for example, lax control of balances held by brokers and agents, or the use of funds to finance the expansion of the business, would be reflected in a smaller yield.

(b) by defining yield in terms of investment earnings instead of income it embraces capital gains, so permitting accurate comparison of companies pursuing different investment policies. Unfortunately in practice this is an unattainable ideal, only details of interest and dividend income being publicly available. Likewise the companies do not publish sufficient information to enable investment earnings to be calculated on a post-tax basis however desirable this may be for present purposes in view of the bearing differences in the tax regulations have on net earnings.

A full-scale test of these three measures of efficiency covering all companies in the British insurance industry over a period of several years would be a massive undertaking. However, a test covering the ten leading non-life companies operating independently in 1966 produced the results which are summarised in figure 7j. It must be emphasised that the results of the individual

149

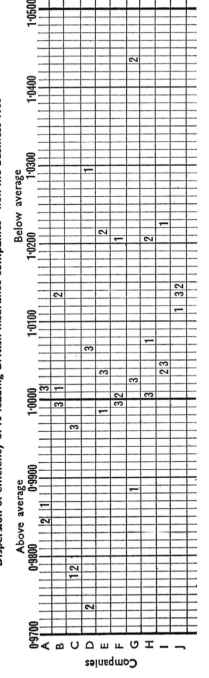

Figure 7j

Dispersion of efficiency of 10 leading British insurance companies—non-life business 1966

Key: 1 = index 1 (underwriting profits/inputs)
      2 = index 2 (underwriting inputs/output)
      3 = index 3 (financial efficiency)

companies were compared with those for the group and not with the industry as a whole.

It would be rash to attempt to draw firm conclusions from such a limited test which omitted the results of the large number of smaller companies, was based on only one year's results and which suffers from the shortcomings of published data mentioned above. Nevertheless two features of the results merit comment. First, though there is a tendency for the results to cluster around the mean there are some notable exceptions. Secondly only one company (C) produced consistently above-average results, and three (H, I and J) were below average in all three areas of performance. The wide dispersion of the results of the two companies D and G is particularly interesting; D had an above-average output/input ratio but produced the worst profit/input performance as measured by index 1, whereas G produced the reverse results. Does this mean that D was looking for growth at any cost while G placed its emphasis on profitability even at the expense of the under-utilisation of its capacity? Before any attempt is made to answer these and other questions it would be desirable to supplement the analysis with more information and to extend the analysis over another couple or so years. Nevertheless figure 7j does at least point to matters meriting further investigation, and would provide the management of an individual company with an insight into the efficiency of both its own and competitors' operations.

Although attention has been concentrated on only one of the nine measures of performance listed on pages 141-142, it is hoped that sufficient has been said to provide the reader with a critical appreciation of the manner in which the problems of inter-company comparison can be tackled, besides indicating some of the more important limitations in published data. Whether one is concerned with efficiency, profits, premium levels or other aspects of performance, the desirability of obtaining data spread over several years cannot be emphasised too strongly. This is particularly true of many classes of non-life insurance where the results for any one particular year may be distorted substantially by the occurrence of some unexpected contingency such as a major catastrophe or a change of law which creates or makes more onerous liabilities which insurers have underwritten.

The larger the volume of objective information available and the higher the standards of analysis, the greater the scope for informed and accurate policy decisions by both insurance managements and regulatory authorities. It is hoped that the foregoing pages have demonstrated in a small way the part that economic analysis can play in that process.

SUGGESTED ADDITIONAL READING

Chapter 1

J. Dunning "Insurance in the British economy", Institute of Economic Affairs (1971).

Economist Intelligence Unit "Insurance: profile of an industry" Corporation of Insurance Brokers (1971).

Chapter 2

W. Horrigan "Risk, risk management, and insurance", Withdean Publications (1969).

H. S. Denenberg and others "Risk and insurance" Prentice Hall (1964).

K. Urban "The economic role of insurance", Report of Inter-regional Seminar on Insurance and Reinsurance 1969, United Nations Conference on Trade and Development.

Chapter 3

G. Clayton and W. T. Osborn "Insurance company investment", Allen and Unwin (1965).

G. M. Dickinson "Determinants of insurance company assets choice", Withdean Publications (1971).

L. D. Jones "Investment policies of life companies", Harvard University Press (1968).

"The financial institutions", Bank of England Quarterly Bulletin, Vol. 10, no. 4, December 1970.

Chapter 4

S. J. Lengyel "International insurance transactions", Wadley and Ginn (1953).

Economist Intelligence Unit "Report on insurance costs in the balance of payments of developing countries", United Nations Conference on Trade and Development (1964) ref. E/CONF 46/5.

Chapter 5

R. H. Leftwich "The price system and resource allocation", 3rd edition, chapters 7 and 8, Holt, Rinehart and Winston (1966).

R. G. Lipsey "An introduction to positive economics", 2nd edition, chapters 19-21, Weidenfeld and Nicholson (1966).

D. C. Hague "Managerial economics", chapters 5-7, Longmans Green & Co. (1969).

C. I. Savage and J. R. Small "Introduction to managerial economics", chapters 6 and 7, Hutchinson (1967).

Chapter 6

R. H. Leftwich "The price system and resource allocation" 3rd edition, chapters 4-6.

R. G. Lipsey "An introduction to positive economics" 2nd edition, chapters 7, 14, 15 and 16.

D. C. Hague "Managerial economics", chapter 4.

C. I. Savage and J. R. Small "Introduction to managerial economics", chapter 8.

Chapter 7

R. H. Leftwich "The price system and resource allocation" 3rd edition, chapters 9-12.

R. G. Lipsey "An introduction to positive economics" 2nd edition, chapters 22-29.

D. C. Hague "Managerial economics", chapters 2, 13 and 14.

C. I. Savage and J. R. Small "Introduction to managerial economics", chapters 2, 3, 9 and 10.

BIBLIOGRAPHY

Association of Insurance Managers in Industry & Commerce, Research Group No. 3 "The status & techniques of insurance managers in industry & commerce" (1969).

Assurance Companies Act, 1909.

Assurance Companies Act, 1946.

Bain, J. S., "Barriers to new competition". Harvard University Press (1956).

Bank of England Quarterly Bulletin "The financial institutions", Dec. 1970.

Baumol, W. J., "Business behaviour, value & growth" Macmillan (1959).

Beard, R. E., "Statistics in motor insurance" Journal of Chartered Insurance Institute, vol. 64, (1967).

Beard, R. E., "Some thoughts on the solvency of insurance companies" Jubilee number of the Quarterly letter of the Algemeene Reinsurance Companies, vol. 1, July 1964.

Berman, L. S., "Role of the personal sector in the flow of funds in the United Kingdom" Economic Trends, November 1969.

Campbell, A. C. "Insurance & Crime", G. P. Putnam's Sons (1902).

Carter, R. L., "Competition in the British fire & accident insurance market" Unpublished D.Phil thesis, University of Sussex (1968).

Carter, R. L., "The watchdog grows up", Policy Holder Insurance Journal 26 July 1968.

Carter, R. L., "Prospects for captives", Policy Holder Insurance Journal, 31 July 1970.

Clark, J. B., "Insurance & Business Profit", Quarterly Journal of Economics, vol. 7, 1892.

Clayton, G., & Osborn, W. T., "Insurance Company Investment", Allen & Unwin (1965).

Committee on Invisible Exports "Britain's invisible earnings" British National Export Council (1967).

Committee on the Working of the Monetary System, The report of Cmnd. 827, HMSO (1959).

Companies Act, 1967.

Consumer Council, "Insurance. A Consumer Council Study" (1970).

Dickinson, G. M., "Determinants of insurance company asset choice" Withdean Publications (1971).

Dickson, P. G. M., "The Sun Insurance Office 1710-1960" Oxford University Press (1960).

Downie, J., "The competitive process", Duckworth & Co. (1958).

Economists Advisory Group "Financial facilities for small firms" a study directed by Dennis Lees. Research report No. 4 of the Committee of Inquiry on Small Firms. HMSO (1971).

Economist Intelligence Unit "Insurance: profile of an industry". Corporation of Insurance Brokers (1971).

Economist Intelligence Unit "Report on insurance costs in the balance of payments of developing countries", United Nations Conference on Trade & Development (1964).

Fama, E. F., "Random walks in stock market prices", Financial Analysts Journal, Sept.-October 1965.

Gibb, D. E. W., "Lloyd's of London", Macmillan & Co. (1957).

Green, P., "Bayesian decision theory in price strategy", Journal of Marketing, 27 January 1963.

Greene, M. R., "Risk & insurance" 2nd edtn. South-Western Publishing Co. (1968).

Hague, D. C., "Managerial Economics", Longmans Green & Co. (1969).

Hammond, J. D., (ed). "Essays in the theory of risk & insurance", Scott, Foresman & Co. (1968).

Hammond, J. S., "Better decisions with preference theory", Harvard Business Review. November-December 1967.

Hauser, M. M., & Burrows, P., "The economics of unemployment insurance", Allen & Unwin (1969).

Hensley, R. J., "Competition, regulation & the public interest in non-life insurance". University of California Press (1962).

Hey, G. B., "Statistics & non-life insurance" vol. 133, Part 1, 1970. Series A (General), Journal of the Royal Statistical Society.

Houston, D. B., "Risk, insurance & sampling" in "Essays in the theory of risk & insurance" ed J. D. Hammond.

Johnston, J. "Statistical cost analysis" McGraw Hill (1960).

Kimball, S. L. & Jackson, B. A., "The regulation of insurance marketing" in "Essays in insurance regulation" (1966).

King, M. H. R., "British insurance & the Common Market" Policy, vol. 70, May 1971.

Knight, F. C., "Insurance productivity" Journal of Chartered Insurance Institute vol. 61 (1964).

Knight, F. H., "Risk, uncertainty & profit" (1921) reprinted by Harper & Row (1965).

Lavington, F., "The English capital market" Methuen & Co. (1921).

Leftwich, "The price system & resource allocation" 3rd edtn., Holt, Rinehart & Winston (1966).

Lengyel, S. J., "International insurance transactions", Wadley & Ginn (1953).

Lengyel, S. J., "Insurance accounts: an economic interpretation & analysis", F. W. Cheshire Pty. Ltd. (1947).

Lipsey, R. J., "An introduction to positive economics" 2nd ed. Weidenfeld & Nicholson (1966).

Little, Arthur D. Inc., "Prices & profits in the property and liability insurance industry". American Insurance Association (1967).

Longley-Cook, L. H., "Rate-making—manual rates" in "Multiple line insurers. Their nature & operation" ed. by G. F. Michelbacher & N. R. Roos, 2nd ed. McGraw Hill (1970).

McDonnell, J. M., "Manpower with special reference to branch organisation" Chartered Insurance Institute 1971 Annual Conference Papers.

Markovitz, H. M., "Portfolio selection: efficient diversification of investments" J. Wiley & Sons (1959).

Morrah, D., "A history of industrial life assurance" Allen & Unwin (1955).

Mowbray, A. H., & Blanchard, R. H., "Insurance" 5th edtn., McGraw Hill (1959).

Neave, J. A. S., "Current problems of the reinsurance market", Policy Holder Insurance Journal, 5 February 1971.

Pfeffer, I., "Insurance & economic theory", R. D. Irwin Inc. (1956).

Plymen, J. & Pullan, S., "Insurance profitability, past, present & future". Journal of Chartered Insurance Institute, vol. 66 (1969).

Rayner, A. C., & Little, J. M. D., "Higgledy Piggledy Growth Again", Blackwell (1966).

Raynes, H. E., "A history of British Insurance" 2nd edtn., Pitman (1964).

Reynolds, D. I. W., "Motor insurance rate fixing", Institute of Actuaries Students' Society (1970).

Richardson, H. J., "Economic theory", Hutchinson (1964).

Simon, H. A., "Theories of decision-making in economics", American Economic Review, June 1959.

Stevens, P. J., "Fatal Aircraft Accidents" the Criminologist, vol. 4, no. 12, May 1969.

Supple, "The Royal Exchange Assurance", Cambridge University Press (1970).

Sweezy, P. M., "Demand under conditions of oligopoly", in "Readings in price theory", American Economic Association, R. D. Irwin (1952).

Swiss Reinsurance Co. "An international comparison of the development of the gross national product, of private and state consumption as well as private expenditure on insurance 1955-1968". Sigma, April 1971.

Swiss Reinsurance Co. "The long-term growth of insurance and the national economy", Sigma, October 1968.

Titmuss, R., "The irresponsible society" in "Essays on theWelfare State", 2nd edtn., Allen & Unwin (1958).

Tobin, J., "Liquidity preference as behaviour toward risks", Review of Economic Studies, vol. 25, February 1958).

Urban, K., "The economic role of insurance" in the report of the inter-regional seminar on Insurance & Reinsurance 1969, United Nations Conference on Trade & Development.

Vaughan, D. G., "Engineering" in "Multiple-line insurers. Their nature & operation", ed. G. F. Michelbacher & N. R. Roos, 2nd edtn, McGraw Hill (1970).

Weber, J. P., "Realism in rating" Journal of Chartered Insurance Institute, vol. 63 (1966).

Willett, A. H., "The theory of risk and insurance" 1901, reprinted by University of Pensylvania Press (1951).

Williams, C. A., "Price discrimination in property and liability insurance". University of Minnesota Press (1959).

INDEX

156

NOTES

NOTES

NOTES